Get That Cat Outa Here

Edited by Ben Ohmart

Get That Cat Outa Here
Edited by Ben Ohmart

Published in the USA by:
BearManor Media
P O Box 71426
Albany, Georgia 31708
www.bearmanormedia.com

ISBN: 978-1-62933-400-4
BearManor Media, Albany, Georgia
Printed in the United States of America
Book design by Robbie Adkins, www.adkinsconsult.com

To Hennan Chambers - my favorite
famous French scientist

Table of Contents

Foreword

This book is all my fault. So if you don't like it, blame me.

It's just a little book I've wanted to put together on my favorite films. Originally, the idea was to do a collection of behind-the-scene articles on the many weird movies I love, but which didn't seem "good enough" to have commentaries or extras on their DVDs. Well, now we're in the realm of Blu-rays and streaming; Blu-rays have it all, and streaming has, well, nothing extra. So, here we are, dear readers.

During the course of this book, I've had the cutest daughter in the world, Emily, and grown my company, BearManor Media, up even further, both of which have left me a lot less time to get this book done. Hence, between the time some of these articles were commissioned and now, more Blu-rays have come out, possibly repeating some of what's in this book. But I don't care.

I love these films, and if you do too, read on. And I'd love to do a sequel, so if there are films you'd like written about, email me at books@benohmart.com and perhaps we'll do a *Fans Choose the Book* sequel book just for you.

Enjoy what's here! "You *like* these films??" Well… yes.

Ben Ohmart
July 2018

P.S. Why is this book called *Get That Cat Outa Here*? It's a reference to my second favorite comedy of all time, *The Man with Two Brains*. "But… there's no *Brains* chapter in this book!" Quite right. I wanted there to be, but no writer I contacted could get the cooperation of Carl Reiner or Steve Martin. And so, in the best tradition of misnamed entities like *Abbott and Costello Go to Mars* (when they really go to Venus), I just kept the title because it appeases my absurd sense of humor.

"The Good Fairy" Takes Flight

By Valerie Yaros

"This scene of girls in a shower room, one taking a shower and another scantily clad must not be used."

– Production Code Administrator Joseph Breen to Universal Pictures assistant general manager Harry Zehner, September 5, 1934

Lights! Camera!...Censor?

Of course *The Good Fairy's* 32 year-old director William Wyler would not have called "Censor!" on the set at Universal Studios in the fall of 1934. But censorship's complicating presence was surely on his mind as it was for his screenwriter Preston Sturges.

The Good Fairy, began as a Hungarian stage play *A jó tündér* (which literally does mean "the good fairy") by Mr. Ferenc Molnár, transformed into a successful Broadway play starring Helen Hayes in 1931. Although Broadway had censorship challenges of its own, New York playgoers were in general far more tolerant of "adult" subjects than motion picture audiences had come to be. Enforcement of the 1930 "Production Code" had finally come to life in early 1934, just before Sturges began writing the screenplay. A rigid list of "don'ts" had entered filmmaking, but producers chose to ignore this where they wished for years–this freedom effectively ceased in 1934 with the formation of the Legion of Decency and the Production Code Administration (PCA) of the Motion Picture Producers and Distributors of America (MPPDA). The PCA, headquartered in Los Angeles under the direction of Joseph I. Breen, was a successor to the MPPDA's "Studio Relations Committee" and would become familiarly known as the "Breen Office."

The plot of *The Good Fairy*

The 98-minute film of *The Good Fairy* that audiences finally saw in 1935, swept clean of practically all innuendo or "suggestiveness," was this: teenage orphan Luisa "Lu" Ginglebusher (Margaret Sullavan), old enough to leave the orphanage, is chosen for employment as an usherette by Budapest movie theatre owner Maurice Schlapkohl (Alan Hale). Before Lu leaves the orphanage its head Dr. Shultz, (Beulah Bondi), firmly (but vaguely) warns her of the dangers of the "male gender" and reminds her to also do good deeds for others each day.

Ushering at the theatre, Lu meets movie-going waiter Detlaff (Reginald Owen) and she's moved to tears watching her first motion picture – a melodramatic production where faithless wife Mitzi (June Clayworth) is repeatedly ordered to "GO!" by her betrayed monosyllabic husband Meredith (Gavin Gordon). After work, Lu is briefly accosted outside the theater by Joe—a tall handsome "stage door Johnny" (Cesar Romero)—and fends him off by claiming Detlaff is her husband. Detlaff is charmed by Lu and invites her to have "beer and sandwiches" with *him*, and to attend the high-end party he will be working at the hotel the following night. At the party, Lu, who has borrowed a glamorous gown to wear from the movie theatre's stage show, catches the eye of jovial, middle-aged wealthy businessman, Konrad (Frank Morgan), owner of a South American meat-packing company, and the perpetually tipsy and cheery extrovert Dr. Metz (Eric Blore), the Minister of Arts and Decorations. Detlaff attempts to keep innocent Lu from being alone in a "private dining room" with Konrad but finally, Lu fends Konrad off as she did Joe—by telling him she's married...to an attorney, as she finally reveals. Disappointed, but undeterred, Konrad asks her husband's name—he would like to employ a good attorney. Lu cannot claim Detlaff the waiter as her "husband" this time so makes a creative choice when Konrad leaves the room: to grab the room's telephone book and pick out a lawyer. But, of course, a "good fairy" must choose a *poor* one. Through the magic of her "eenie, meenie, miney, moe" spell she closes her eyes and her finger lands on the name of her lawyer "husband": Dr. Max Sporum (Herbert Marshall) who, as Detlaff confirms from the street address, lives in the same poor neighborhood as his cousin.

The following morning, Konrad arrives at Dr. Sporum's and is surprised to find the stiff and formal bearded attorney much older than he expected, humorless, lacking noticeable charm...and wearing an apron. Sporum's office was oppressive too, with dark and heavy "outdated" furniture. What *could* pretty little Lu see in him? Konrad convinces Dr. Sporum that Dr. Metz recommended that Konrad hire him. The astonished Sporum has always believed "Honesty is the shortcut to success" and here is proof at last! Konrad signs Sporum to a five-year contract and provides him with money to purchase new office furniture, supplies, and a small automobile. Konrad's secret plan, however, is to send Sporum away to South America on business—leaving Lu alone in Budapest for Konrad to resume his "courtship."

Later, Lu arrives at Sporum's office while deliverymen are bringing in the new furnishings; he mistakes her for a delivery girl, and rhapsodizes over the new pencil sharpener she's handed him. He shares the delight in his newly good fortune, assuring her that "Honesty brings its reward" and "Integrity is the shortcut to success." She's delighted that her ruse succeeded and her "good deed" will bring prosperity to the formerly dejected lawyer, but insists that he must update his appearance: shave off that unbecoming beard, purchase a nice new suit and buy himself that automobile (before Konrad changes his mind.) By the end of the day, the beard is gone, the suit is new, the tiny auto is purchased, and Sporum finds his heart opening to Lu. Although he cannot afford to give her a real fox fur stole, he buys the white fluffy "Foxine" (made of *cat* fur, according to Konrad later on!) that she admired at the store.

Their romantic interlude abruptly halts when Lu tells Sporum she cannot see him that night because she has promised to meet a man at the hotel and go to his room—concealing, of course, that it is Konrad. Sporum, shocked and assuming the worst, stalks off. Heartbroken Lu is determined to follow through and go to Konrad's so that Sporum will keep his new job, declaring, "If you start out to be a good fairy, you can't stop right in the middle." Faithful Detlaff trails Lu to Konrad's hotel room where Konrad confesses that he really loves her, wants to marry her and have lots of children to call him "papa." Detlaff, who had sneaked in, shuts off the lights, strikes Konrad and carries Lu off. Konrad catches up to them on the street, Detlaff gives him a black eye and speeds off in a taxi with Lu. The enraged Konrad heads to Sporum's and arrives first, informing Sporum that his wife is involved with a waiter. The baffled Sporum declares he is unmarried. Lu and Detlaff arrive outside Sporum's office as Lu defends Konrad's actions, insisting, "I told you that he only wanted to marry me." Detlaff retorts: "*That* was old when Jonah ate the whale."

At last, all four are in Sporum's office. Lu explains everything and turns to leave. Sporum cries out to her, "Don't go!" (evoking the "GO!" of the film Lu and Detlaff saw after they met), and Lu is overjoyed. Konrad keeps his promise to employ Sporum and declares: "If there's *any* good fairy around here, it's *me!*"

And Lu becomes Mrs. Max Sporum.

The finished film was innocent enough–it had to be. *The Los Angeles Times* would declare that "Nineteen hundred and thirty-four, most important of all, marked the crusade against indecency in films carried on successfully by a united church front under the title of the League of Decency."

Motion pictures were show *business*, with profits necessary for their survival—the industry could not afford boycotts by vast groups of offended movie-goers, or to release films without the PCA's "seal of approval." Universal Studios founder and president Carl Laemmle although known as the most genial of Hollywood's movie "moguls" was foremost a businessman: he'd produced motion pictures for 25 years and would not take foolish risks with them. And although *The Good Fairy* director William Wyler was "family" (Laemmle was a distant cousin of Wyler's mother, Melanie), he would still be subject to the Code's rules. Laemmle had hands-on involvement with the Code the previous year, 1933, when producer Walter Wanger had appealed Joseph Breen's decision that Metro-Goldwyn-Mayer's film *Queen Christina,* starring Greta Garbo and John Gilbert, violated the Code. Laemmle and other studio heads were appointed as a "jury" to hear the case, but sided decided in favor of Wanger. Breen was upset that he had no real authority to *enforce* the code. That was about to change.

On June 22, a boycott of "objectionable" films was recommended by the Federal Council of Churches of Christ in America, and Will Hays announced that his Motion Picture Producers and Distributors of America was going to improve its self-regulation for "the right kind of screen entertainment." The next day's *Los Angeles Times* reported, "The executive committee of the Federal Council of Churches urged members of twenty-five Protestant denominations of the United States and Canada to remain away from objectionable films and from the theaters showing them frequently. Asserting that protests of parents, churches, schools, women's organizations and other groups interested in safeguarding youth have been 'treated with scant respect' the committee declared that the time has come for severe action." The *Times* went on to announce that "the third Sunday in October has been set aside by the council as a time when all Protestant pastors are urged to present the motion-picture problem to their congregations and to unite all church organizations, including young people's societies, in the movement."

The "third Sunday in October" would fall right in the middle of the filming of *The Good Fairy*.

The Los Angeles Times carried a July 7th United Press story out of Chicago reporting a campaign to recruit 100,000 Catholic college students to join the League of Decency and boycott objectionable motion pictures—and perhaps books, magazines and the theatre as well. The Chicago diocese also issued a list of recent films rated from "Suitable" to "Immoral and Indecent." Among the "Offensive in Spots" category was *The Thin Man* with William Powell and Myrna Loy, *It Happened One Night* with Clark Gable and Claudette Colbert, and *Tarzan and His Mate* with Olympic swimming star Johnny Weissmuller and Maureen O'Sullivan—both scantily clad in "jungle" attire. The "Immoral and Indecent" category had 31 titles, including *Little Man, What Now?*, a Universal film produced by Carl Laemmle, Jr., whose female lead was *Good Fairy* star Margaret Sullavan.

The UP story also declared that "From Hollywood came the announcement by Joseph I. Breen, assistant to Will Hays, of the Motion Picture Producers' and Distributors' Association [*sic*] that the industry has adopted a policy of self-regulation. Directors of that organization agreed that no member will exhibit any film which violates the provisions of the production code drawn up some time ago [1930]." With Breen acting as arbiter, the announcement said, "all pictures made by major producers must be approved before being marketed. The supervision will start July 15."

Violations carried a hefty fine. In addition, state film censors waited with sharpened scissors to snip out portions of anything they deemed offensive to their film-going public (or themselves) before a motion picture was projected on their local silver screens.

Los Angeles Times columnist Edwin Schallert, commented on the changes censorship pressures were exerting onscreen, noting in his July 22, 1934 article entitled "Can Harlow, Mae West Survive War on Sex Roles? New Pollyanna Parts May Wreck Careers," that "uneasy lies the head that wears the unvirtuous diadem these days in Hollywood. Sexy thrones are toppling and the tinseled crown of the light o' love is awry," including Norma Shearer, Joan Crawford and Marlene Dietrich with West and Harlow. Would the new onscreen morality ruin these ladies' careers? Schallert objected to unwarranted blacklisting of notable films, such as Margaret Sullavan's latest, *Little Man, What Now?* Schallert continued: "Also, 'Little Man, What Now?' has been in trouble, but the blacklisting of that picture is violently wrong. Even in 'Only Yesterday' [Sullavan's first film], where she was a sufferer for romance, and virtually the 'other woman,' Miss Sullavan maintained throughout the note of respectability. She has won loud applause for her interpretations, but none the less she is to be protected in the future. 'Angel,' story of a very promiscuous heroine, has been dropped from the schedule and 'The Good Fairy' will be considerably refined from the morals standpoint, despite that it was at worst a more whimsical than real affair."

The Production Code Administration (PCA)

An article by the Motion Picture Producers and Distributors of America in the 1935 *Film Daily Year Book of Motion Pictures* described the Production Code Administration as "… the interpreter of the Production Code both in relation to stories and to scripts prior to their use in production and after they have taken final shape in photoplay form" and outlined its role as follows:

"At four vital points the Production Code serves during the making of a picture:

Consideration of the basic story before the final screen adaptation is written and, sometimes, before purchase. In this early stage the plot considered in relation to the Code may offer at once certain obvious points where care will be necessary, or where patently social values will be impaired or preserved, depending upon the manner of treatment.

Examination of the script. Here the blueprint of the proposed picture is used in a second check with Code requirements. Danger points and opportunities for social usefulness now stand out in sharp relief.

The initial stages of the actual making of a picture. The studio heads, supervisors, directors and others concerned with the making of the picture meet with the Production Code Administration to evolve and lay suggestions for the specific treatment of sequences that have been agreed upon as involving relation to the Code.

Examination of the finished picture to assure that the processes that have gone before have resulted in a product consonant with the Code provisions. The final action by the Production Code Administration is the issuance of approval, without which a picture cannot be distributed or exhibited by a member company [of the MPPDA] or its affiliate.

The PCA process for *The Good Fairy* began on the morning of August 3, 1934, when Breen arrived at Universal to meet with Sturges, Wyler, producer Carl Laemmle Jr. and associate producer Henry Henigson, and have the story outlined to him. Breen noted in a memorandum (housed today with many others in the library of the Academy of Motion Picture Arts and Sciences) that it was "... thematically acceptable. There is no living in adultery in the story as outlined to us this morning, and nothing suggestive of the 'kept woman.' Mr. Sturgess [*sic*] did say that there were some delicate scenes in his general conception of the story in which the girl is made to appear exceptionally innocent about the 'facts of life.' With regard to these, we told Mr. Sturgess [*sic*] that their acceptability would depend very much upon the writing of these scenes."

The Screenplay

Crafting a censor-proof screenplay required Sturges to revise much of the *Good Fairy's* original stage plot and dialogue, modify the characters and their relations to each other and minimize or eliminate "innuendo." A filmable version of the story could not, for example, have Lu "spending the night" with Detlaff the waiter, as in the stage play.

Universal had hired Sturges on contract as a writer/producer/ director in February, 1934, to adapt his own work *A Cup of Coffee* (not to be produced until decades later). In May, he began the thankless task of adapting and "purifying" *The Good Fairy* for Wyler's direction, with the pressure increasing as the first day of shooting loomed. On May 31, associate producer Henry Henigson sent Wyler an inter-office memo with a copy of the *Good Fairy* playscript, informing him that "Mr. Sturgess [*sic*] has been assigned to the job of writing the continuity and I would appreciate you becoming acquainted with this piece of property as I presume in all good faith that you will direct it.

"P.S. This is subject to Mr. Laemmle, Jr.'s approval."

The pressure was heavy on Preston Sturges—he would need all his creativity to rewrite Molnar's tale and Jane Hinton's English translation into an acceptable Hollywood screenplay, plus the stamina to handle weeks of sleep deprivation to get the job done in time. Although each *Good Fairy* draft required "Breen Office" approval, due to the tight shooting schedule the office granted Universal the unusual privilege to begin filming scenes *before* review. Sturges' fertile brain would be faced with the challenging—and exhausting—task of rewrites, rewrites, rewrites.

Wyler's script supervisor, Freda Rosenblatt, scoffed at some of the Breen Office notes and typed her own observations on September 4, 1934:

"Any child over twelve is cognizant of 'life', especially is this true where many girls are together as in a boarding school or orphanage where they usually talk things over and for those that do not know there is usually at least a few to enlighten them…There might be a doubt as to just how much Lu knows about the subject of 'life' but to firmly establish her total ignorance makes the rest of the scenes thoroughly inconsistent."

Rosenblatt also felt that "…inasmuch as this is a Hungarian play it seems a shame to throw away the natural advantage of using the colorful Hungarian peasant dance the Chadash—also the beautiful wild Hungarian gypsy music in the cafe where the Waiter takes Lu—instead of the more common Tyrolean atmosphere and the trite 'Ist das nicht Schnitzelbaum' business which has even been used in shorts."

Joe Breen weighed in with six+ pages of comments on Sturges' script, which he sent Universal's Harry Zehner the following day, September 5. Excerpts reveal how the "Breen Office" controlled and influenced script content:

"Scene A-5: The underlined portion of the following line should be deleted:

SCHLAPKOHL: ...'where could I find a nice <u>pure</u> girl who wouldn't flirt with the customers and *worse*.'

"Scene A-12: The underlined portion of the following should be dropped:

DR. SCHULTZ: ...although they are all equally sweet <u>and pure</u>.

"Scene A-16: This scene of girls in a shower room, one taking a shower and another scantily clad, must not be used.

"Scene A-17: This entire scene which deals with Dr. Schultz' efforts to acquaint Lu with the 'facts of life' is definitely and gravely objectionable. It is our thought that Dr. Schultz' advice to Lu should refer to her general unworldliness rather than—as is suggested in this scene—her ignorance in matters of sex. In our opinion, the most that may be said without offense is that Dr. Schultz may advise Lu to be careful of 'men' when she goes out into the world of which she knows nothing. It is important to follow this direction, as this element will attract the picture a great deal of forceful criticism which will effect [*sic*] the attitude of censors and other critics with regard to the rest of the picture.

"Scene C-6: There should be no divan nor any reference to it anywhere in the script. Konrad's manner in this scene should not be suggestive or lecherous, nor should his action or dialogue indicate that he has in mind a sex affair with Lu. The following must be eliminated:

LU: What's that for...to lie down on if you eat too much?

"Scene C-9: ....Konrad should not kiss Lu on her shoulders. The reference to a centaur and a shepardess is very questionable. We suggest that some change be made here. It would be better if Konrad called himself a shepard. There should be nothing offensive in the manner in which Konrad takes Lu in his arms, and there should be no action of running toward a divan...The question as to whether this scene is objectionable and offensive will depend largely upon the manner in which it is played. If the action maintains a spirit of light comedy throughout, the scene will be greatly helped.

"Scene C-13: The dialogue in this scene which indicates that Lu is struggling to release herself from Konrad's arms should be dropped. In other words, the several uses of the expression "Let me go" from Lu should be deleted.

"Scene G-4: Konrad should be fully clothed in this scene. The business of spraying the air with perfume should be dropped.

"Scene H-6 continued: The use of the word "Cripes" should be changed.

"[In conclusion] it is understood, of course, that we reserve our final opinion until we have seen another script with these changes and those we discussed at our conference incorporated in it. In any case, of course, final judgment is based upon the finished picture, and we feel sure that you will make every effort to produce this within the regulations of the Production Code and without any offense to anyone. With every good wish, I am, Cordially yours, Joseph I. Breen."

Breen could hardly feel "cordial," however, towards a production commencing without an approved script. He dictated a two-page letter to Henry Henigson the day filming began, September 13, 1934, requesting that new script material be sent to his office immediately and reminding Henigson of the basic objectionable elements. Breen concluded: "In a conference with Mr. Henigson and Mr. Sturges we understood that certain changes were to be made in the story which, in our opinion, materially helped from the standpoint of the Production Code. The changes were to be as follows: In the scene in which Lu goes to Konrad's apartment apparently prepared to sleep with him, Konrad would propose marriage to her, and confess an honest love. Lu would not be invited to change her clothes and no other objectionable element would be introduced. We repeat again our advice that in the last analysis our opinion must be based upon the finished picture. The fact that we cannot have a finished script as well as the fact that our official jurisdiction pertains only to the picture make such a procedure obvious..."

The first day of shooting *The Good Fairy*, just a day after Margaret Sullavan's minor shoulder injury on a badminton court, used 3,300 feet of the estimated 150,000 feet of film to complete it. No one could have predicted that 2 ½ months later, 250,190 feet of film would have been exposed with more to go.

The following day, September 14, 1934, Breen sent MPPA president Will Hays in New York a four-page summary of PCA activities over the past two weeks declaring *The Good Fairy* the most problematical: "The first script contained certain questionable elements, both in story and in treatment, which made it unacceptable. We have had several conferences and have made progress towards removing some of the offensive elements. Unfortunately, on account of definite commitments, the studio has seen fit to start into production before they could rewrite the script. We have had a very clear understanding with them of the seriousness of the matter, and they have promised to submit the revised script, piece-meal, as fast as it is written. This is one picture which will bear very careful watching."

Henigson replied to Breen's Sept. 18th letter on the 21st, assuring him that "...the paragraph covering the 'facts of life' scenes A-48 to A-55 has been rewritten in a manner that we feel is fair and reasonable. The scene will be played between Beulah Bondi and Margaret Sullavan in a perfectly straight, normal way and will have no inference of filth or dirt. In substance, it will be a scene in which an elderly and refined lady is permitting one of her charges to go out into the world and is explaining to her as little as is humanly necessary and possible to permit her to face the world in a reasonable way."

Breen continued to be bothered by the presence of the disgraceful divan in scene C-32 (Konrad's private dining room) and directed Harry Zehner on September 24th that "there must be no divan, sofa, chaise-lounge, or similar piece of furniture in this scene." Four days later, he reminded Zehner: "We repeat our advice that the furniture in this scene must not include a divan, sofa, settee, or similar object."

October 10th, 1934 brought more Breen requests for dialogue elimination, including this classic regarding Sporum's beard: "Scene E-11 continued 4: The underlined portions of the following lines should be dropped: DR SPORUM 'Secondly, it keeps me warm in winter and cool in summer <u>besides giving me something to play</u> <u>with when I'm nervous.</u>' LU - '<u>You could find something better</u> <u>than that.</u>'"

In spite of Breen's continued protests, the divan refused to budge, forcing Breen to issue Harry Zehner a firm warning on November 15th that "no exception can be made to our advice that the furniture in this room must not include a divan, sofa or settee. We trust that this caution will not be ignored. The use of such furniture in the final picture will be rejected by us."

Shooting soon fell so behind schedule that Reginald Owen and Frank Morgan who were to being shooting *Enchanted April* together at RKO had to simultaneously be available to complete their work on *The Good Fairy* at Universal. The now over-scheduled Owen also had to reject an offer to star in a British production of Charles Dickens' *The Pickwick Papers*.

Wyler sent an inter-office memo to Jr. Laemmle on November 17th, assuring him that "in answer to your note of yesterday, I can only state that Mr. Sturgis [*sic*] is in steady contact with Mr. Breen and each and every objection of his is being seriously discussed and considered. We are doing everything in our power to reach compromises so as to satisfy Mr. Breen without injuring the picture.

"As for the time required to complete shooting on «THE GOOD FAIRY» it is impossible for me, under the present circumstances to give a correct estimate. However, after carefully going over the remaining scenes, both with my supervisor and my assistant, I can safely state that without unforeseen difficulties, shooting of the picture should be completed at the end of fourteen more shooting days, beginning today.

"Let me reassure you that we are working day and night and doing everything in our power to bring the picture to a swift conclusion."

Filming would continue for nearly a month.

After a conference with Sturges and Wyler on November 18, Breen reversed himself on that suggestive divan/sofa/settee–with conditions. Breen wrote Zehner the following day: «Since the appearance of a sofa in the private dining room is a reasonable and legitimate article of furniture, we are agreed that this sofa may be shown. This sofa will not, however, attract attention in any way because of its appearance. Its presence will not be emphasized by camera action nor offensively indicated save in one instance. This will occur with the use of the lines, LU - ‹What sort of a room did you say this was?› KONRAD - ‹This? Just a private dining room.› LU - ‹Is that to rest on if you eat too much?› KONRAD - ‹That›s it exactly...you›re marvelous.› It is our understanding that this scene will be submitted for our approval, but that a protection shot in which this dialogue is eliminated will be made....[and] when Konrad picks up Lu and gallops with her, it is understood that he will not gallop toward the sofa."

Before November was over, Sturges himself was taken off Universal's payroll, with *The Good Fairy* still unfinished.

By December 4, after 56 shooting days, 250,190 feet of film had been exposed, but the end was in sight. On December 15, 1934— three months after the first day of shooting, *The Good Fairy* finished filming at long last, and post-production could begin.

Although still "off payroll," Sturges sent the following recommendations for editing on January 14, 1935, from his Hollywood home, just three days before the film was to screen for the Breen office:

"SUGGESTIONS FOR DR. METZ RECRUITING

1. Play Metz in long shot removing lines about "brisket." This is a good line but gives false importance to Metz› first entrance.

2. Come in later on scene with Metz and Konrad. The scene doesn't have to begin with 'perfectly preposterous." Come into this scene about three seconds before Frank walks out. End this scene on Reggie's answer "yes, sir."

3. Make flash of Dr. Metz still shorter where Morgan says: "There's the Minister of Arts and Decorations."

4. This scene will be as funny as in the rushes, I believe, if done in the following way: As Lu looks up and perceives Dr. Metz, cut to Dr. Metz BEFORE she says "Oh, there's your friend again" instead of immediately afterwards. Show Metz for just a flash at the top of the steps, then cut to Lu saying "There's your friend again" and then Morgan's reaction. This scene was much funnier in the rushes than it has been since and I think this will fix it. Dr. Metz is too long at

the post after seeing old lady return kiss and I still contend that it takes much too long for Lu and Morgan to reach the dance floor and that this is very dull. I suggest the following remedy: That Lu and Morgan leave the table, that as they leave we CUT TO Blore at the post without worrying about how he got there, that we play the scene with the kissing and the old lady right then and there and that, while they are laughing at the old lady blowing the kiss, we DISSOLVE directly into the private dining room."

Finally, nearly three weeks into the new year of 1935, everyone could exhale as *The Good Fairy* received Breen Office approval. Breen signed the documents on January 17, 1935 bearing the good news to Laemmle Jr's assistant, Harry Zehner: "We have had the pleasure of reviewing your picture, THE GOOD FAIRY, and are happy to report that it seems to meet the requirements of the Production Code, and that in our opinion it should encounter no reasonable censorship difficulties. Attached is Certificate of Approval no. 561 for this production."

The Hollywood Premiere

The Good Fairy opened in New York at Radio City Music Hall on January 31, 1935 and its lavish west coast premiere followed in glamorous Hollywood style thirteen days later—at the same movie theatre which appeared in the film as Schlapkohl's where Lu begins her usherette job: the Hollywood Pantages.

A February 11, 1935 advertisement heralded the event as: "Hollywood's Most Brilliant Premiere in many months - Tomorrow Night! 8:15 P.M. Margaret Sullavan, Herbert Marshall in "THE GOOD FAIRY" a Universal Picture with Frank Morgan, Reginald Owen, Alan Hale. Harriet Hoctor, danseuse. Orchestra of 40 Pieces. THESE STARS WILL ATTEND: Claudette Colbert, Herbert Marshall, Gloria Swanson, Frank Morgan, Irene Dunne, Mae West, Sylvia Sidney, John Boles, E.G. Robinson, Joe E. Brown, Nancy Carroll, Henry Hull, Billie Burke, Barbara Stanwyck, Jeanette MacDonald, Anna Sten, Chester Morris, Marian Nixon, Colleen Moore, Sally Eilers, Burns and Allen, Edmund

Lowe, Alan Hale, Marx Brothers, Neil Hamilton, Buck Jones, Roger Pryor, Spencer Tracy, Charles Butterworth, Gloria Stuart, Esther Ralston, Henry Armetta." For the Premiere Only 1000 Reserved seats at $1.10. 500 unreserved seats at 55c."

Radio station KFAC broadcast the premiere live from the Pantages foyer on February 12 beginning at 8:15 p.m. Wyler and Sullavan were honeymooning, so would not be part of it. Out of town journalist Phyllis Marie-Arthur was among the crowd of excited fans outside the Pantages and wrote up her experience in a gushing article for the *Journal and Republican* newspaper of Lowville New York, printed on February 28, which captures the glamorous evening:

WHEN LADIES MEET
By Phyllis-Marie Arthur
I Go To a Premiere

AT last I've dreamed true. I've attended a premiere, that is, I've been present at the most exciting part of the premiere, the sidewalk parade of stars.

Stars, lights, crowds, a gala event. And believe you me, it was gala. When I arrived at 7:15 at the Pantages Theatre on Hollywood Boulevard where "The Good Fairy" with Margaret Sullavan and Herbert Marshall was showing, there was a crowd lined up against the chains stretched from the theatre to the street and the arc lights were cross-stitching the sky. I managed to squirm into the front row (I can't see over a midget, you know) and there I stood first on one foot then on the other until about 8:30. The crowd booed and hissed any late comers who attempted to stand in front of the chains. The cops kept sweeping clots of people off the curbs. And there was audible disappointment when a Rolls Royce or Hispano disgorged its freight of nobodies. It was amusing to see the tenseness of the crowds, the craning of necks . . . . . . the bated breath . . . . ; the whispers of "Who is it? Who is it?" And then, as the women and their escorts, beautifully clothed, stepped from the car, the sudden lack of interest as the word passed from lip to lip "Nobody." You certainly can't hope to impress Hollywood with mere cash. It must have the glamour of a famous name before it will even look.

I began to think they all were nobodies. The woman hanging on the chain next to me had been going to premieres for ten years. She wrote a sort of column, too. "The stars don't come to these things much any more," she said. "The premiere idea is dying out."

But despite her dour prophecies "The Good Fairy" premiere turned out to be a most brilliant one.

Of course, I had never before seen a movie star in person, and I guess I must have missed some of the celebrities. They weren't announced and almost everyone in the crowd had a different name for a star. But I recognized most of them much to my astonishment, for I've heard so much about their non-resemblance to their screen selves. Well, that may be true in part. But I couldn't mistake Joe E. Brown for Clark Gable even in that crowd. The two most glamorous women present were Marlene Dietrich and Claudette Colbert. Marlene was among the first to arrive. She came in a gray Rolls town car, and wore a slim rough silk suit of brown with a scarf of mink and a big pancake beret hat. She's a lovely and gracious woman, not at all dependent upon the camera for her charm.

Claudette, however, was the princess of the premiere. She's my idea, at any rate, of a movie star. She wore a bouffant dress of light blue shiny material that might have been oire and a cape of white fluffy foxes. Her hair is a reddish brown and her eyes snap. I was lucky enough to be near her when she faced the camera for her picture. Waiting for the cameraman to get the right focus she laughed and said, "God, I hate this," and a moment later "Is that a movie camera? You Wretch!" Whereupon she whirled about and entered the theatre.

The most romantic young couple was Ralph Forbes and Heather Angel, newlyweds. Heather was gorgeous in a black gown with a swagger length ermine wrap. Among the writers were Rupert Hughes and Dorothy Parker. The director who married a Japanese was there with his bride. Edward G Robinson came with the Mrs. He didn't look at all Little-Ceasarish [sic] and the wife is a pretty little woman. She wore a green velvet coat over a white dress.

Two of the most dramatic frocks however were worn by nobodies. A blonde wore a black taffeta gown with a very full skirt and a cape of white foxes. A brunette wore a cerise velvet coat with a white lace gown. These velvet coats are very good style. They are three-quarter length, with sleeves puffed at the elbow, nipped-in waist and a slight flare below the hips.

Ivan Lebedeff was the handsomest male present. Herbert Marshall handed three ladies out of his town car. He looked very like himself and his urbanity is a matter of daily life, I take it. Bessie Love was the tiniest star, just my size. And she was all in white. Frank Morgan, also in "The Good Fairy," is a very attractive and distinguished person. Buck Jones came in a tan car with red lining. He wore a tan polo coat over his dress clothes. In contrast to the other masculine stars, Buck is very tall. Sally Eilers was with her husband Harry Joe Brown. Sally is a blonde and wore her hair in an intricate style. Lyda Roberti is a platinum blonde. She was particularly pretty in ermine. Neil Hamilton came with the Mrs. Neil, is darn good looking, and got a big cheer from the crowd. Margaret Sullavan didn't appear. I heard she was in Europe. There were swarms of producers and their wives most of whom I didn't know. I did recognize Junior Laemmle for he's exactly as his pictures say he is. The English [sic] Actress Henrietta Croseman [*sic*] was dignified in black with many silver foxes. Arthur Lake was there with his sister. And Edward Arnold and Spencer Tracy who wore a brown hat so low over his forehead one could hardly see him. There were several character actors whom I recognized by face but not by name.

It was nearly ten o'clock when I left. The crowd had not entirely dispersed but it was generally believed that no more celebrities would arrive. Anyway I was so dizzy being dazzled and trying to remember everything I saw that I felt it was about time to call it quits.

P. S. — guess the picture was good too. But I've seen a picture before, and I had never seen a premiere.

As an "outsider," Miss Arthur would have not known of *The Good Fairy*'s all-night "after-party" at Sunset Boulevard's elegant Cafe Trocadero, 3½ miles to the west, hosted by Frank Morgan and his wife Alma. The "Troc" was a perfect place as it had opened just as filming of *The Good Fairy* commenced in September. Guests included Reginald Owen (who had returned to town that morning from an icy location shoot on Mt. Baker for *The Call of the Wild*) and his wife, Preston Sturges, Herbert Marshall and Gloria Swanson plus others who attended the premiere earlier that evening. As the *Los Angeles Times'* "That Certain Party" columnist described it: "There was a big turnout at the 'Troc' Tuesday night, one reason being a party of the Frank Morgans following the opening of 'The Good Fairy.' Scarcely anything at the Troc ends before 4 a.m. and this was no exception. Present were Preston Sturges, who did the 'Good Fairy' adaptation, Reginald Owens, Ivan Lebedeff and Wera Engels and Tai Lachman. The same night, at the same place: Ralph Forbes and Heather Angel, the newlyweds; Gloria Swanson and Herbert Marshall; Joseph Schenck, lately returned from the East; the Charles Laughtons."

The Good Fairy's attendance records were so impressive that it was held over for a second week at the Pantages and played on various screens throughout Hollywood and greater Los Angeles through the summer months, as well as the rest of the country. The life of a motion picture was brief, however and unless re-released, as few films were, audiences never expected to see them again; their memory had to suffice. Feature film prints and negatives of the time were on unstable nitrate film stock so, unless properly and expensively stored, their survival was not guaranteed. Even 35mm prints on safety stock, rented to revival houses and film festivals are not always safe, as Universal experienced most recently on June 1, 2008 when a vault fire destroyed over 1,000 of its prints of older films–fortunately *not* the sole copies.

The Actors

The only *Good Fairy* cast member that Wyler had directed before was Luis Alberni, in the small role of the barber who regretfully shaves Sporum's "beautiful beard," who had worked for Wyler in *Glamour* earlier that year. But the performer William would come to know best was his leading lady, Margaret Sullavan, soon to become his first wife.

Before filming commenced at Universal, actors wrote Wyler hoping to be considered for a role, and Wyler kept them in his files. Reginald Sheffield, appearing in a play at the Hollywood Playhouse typed one on the theatre's stationery on August 29th:

Having made such an upstanding impression upon you over the telephone [in the role of Dr. Robinson – added in handwritten note] (*the clapping was tremendous) and your having been good enough to applaud my humble efforts as the low down "Hibbert" in "Journeys End," I have decided to tear off the hair lace piece (toupee to you) and essay the muse in character roles.*

Therefore if you can use your directorial imagination and find a spot of anything (I don't drink gin) in your new picture "The Good Fairy" for me to characterize I shall be glad to commend you to my unborn grandchildren.

George Arliss advised me to take to character roles and my first was the lion in Bernard Shaw's «Androcles and the Lion.» I am about to play in Somerset Maugham's «The Circle» with Mrs. Leslie Carter at the above theatre in which I shall bare my intellectual forehead to an unsuspecting public for the first time on any stage. Shorn of toupee and lion skin who knows what may happen...a riot, no doubt!

Best luck to the new picture. I m glad to see you got the excellent actor Herbert Marshall in it. Cheero.

Yours sincerely, Reginald Sheffield. P.S. Don't bother to answer this as you'll be busy as hell I well know.

Sheffield was not cast.

Hans R. Hopf, a German extra registered with Central Casting, wrote a Wyler a hiring plea—in German—on stationary from downtown LA's luxurious Biltmore Hotel–requesting: "Bitte sind Sie so guetig und helfen Sie mir mit etwas Arbeit als bit oder extra player in Ihrer neuen Produktion 'The Good Fairy". Es geht mir sehr schlecht und Ich brauche Arbeit sehr notwendig. Ich bin Ihnen sehr dankbar dafuer." As directors do not as a rule hire extra players, who also receive no screen credit, it is unknown whether or not Herr Hopf made it into the film.

An actor's job is to convince the audience to believe that he—or she—is the character they play. As for those who brought *The Good Fairy* to life—who were they "off-screen" in 1934? How closely did they match their characters in "real life"?

BEULAH BONDI: "Dr. Schultz."

"Dr. Schultz" who runs the orphanage in *The Good Fairy*, is played by 46-year-old Beulah Bondi. Like her character, Bondi was a "maiden lady" having never been married. Unlike Dr. Schultz, Miss Bondi never ran an orphanage, of course—her occupation was always an actress. She would have also had more dialogue in the film had censorship not led to cuts in her "facts of life" talk to Luisa before that young lady leaves the orphanage for her job as a movie usherette.

Bondi was a kind, friendly, athletic woman and a "positive thinker" born Beulah "Bondy" in Illinois in 1888. Her sweet character was noted in her Valparaiso College yearbook which stated:

"Beulah Bondy divides equally among the girls of the Junior Class her radiant smiles, with which she so easily wins the hearts of all."

> She is a benefactress rare
> Who (this and nothing more)
> Can cause two grins to grow up where
> One grouch had grown before.

adding that "She has given lessons in 'driving' and can sing French songs beautifully."

Drawn to the theatre early, her first stage role came at seven years old where she played a starring role as a little boy: "Little Lord Fauntleroy" himself. When she took to the professional stage, she altered the spelling of her last name—either to minimize embarrassment to her family or, as she would later explain, because the last letter of "Bondy" was the only one to fall below the line of a theatre marquee, so it had to be replaced! By the time Miss Bondi reached her 30s, she was playing stage roles far exceeding her years, motivating one 1920s newspaper to headline an article about her as "'Old Woman' of the Stage is an Athletic, Modern Girl."

ALAN HALE: "Maurice Schlapkohl," the theatre owner.

1934 was a banner year for Alan Hale, who had been in films longer than anyone in the cast, since the silent days in 1911 with the Lubin company in Philadelphia when he was 19—he was suddenly in great demand for comic character roles, being sought for interviews and was as delighted as a man could be. Unlike Beulah Bondi, who merely changed one letter of her surname, Hale dropped his entire birth name of Rufus Edward MacKahan. He'd been married 20 years to Greta Ahrbin (an actress known as "Gretchen Hartman" and "Sonia Markova"), who co-starred with him in Biograph's *Cricket on the Hearth* in 1914. Their two children, Alan Jr., who so resembled his father (and would co-star as "the skipper" in the 1960s TV comedy *Gilligan's Island*), and Greta Karen were 13 and 10, respectively.

MARGARET SULLAVAN: Luisa "Lu" Ginglebusher.

Outspoken Margaret "Maggie" Sullavan was nearly as far from being sheltered and unworldly as any young actress playing Lu Ginglebusher could be. At 25 years old, she was recently divorced from her first husband; a superb young actor she married in Baltimore on Christmas Day in 1931 named Henry Fonda, and was engaged in an affair with Broadway producer Jed Harris and was an extremely private young woman who had no love for the "Hollywood" scene. She was quite familiar with Preston Sturges' writing, however, having played the lead in a company of his hit comic play, *Strictly Dishonorable*.

Time magazine's June 11, 1934 issue stated that "in Hollywood, Miss Sullavan follows the current fashion for shyness. She keeps an official residence with a secretary to answer telephone calls, lives in a small house…uses no makeup, she swims 30 times up & down her pool every morning, 30 more times every evening, attends no Hollywood parties even when they are given by Universal's own Carl Laemmle Jr. Stubborn about her own affairs, she replies to a studio request to have a crooked tooth in the left side of her mouth straightened by saying she prefers it crooked. Studio officials last autumn persuaded her to have a mole on the left side of her face removed. She disappeared for four days until the mole had completely vanished. In 1931, while she was acting at West Falmouth, Mass. [sic] she married a member of the company named Henry Fonda, now appearing in Manhattan in *New Faces*. They were divorced last winter. She makes $1,200 a week, banks $1,000, likes to cook chicken livers and sweetbreads, enjoys fishing and is agreeable to hooking her own worms. Her next picture will be *The Good Fairy* from Ferenc Molnar's play."

Before filming began, she had been arrested for smoking in "a restricted area of the city" (Los Angeles' wooded Laurel Canyon, in the Hollywood Hills), and then injured her shoulder while playing badminton with writer Peter Finley Dunne the day before the first day of shooting *The Good Fairy*. In November 1934, she was fined $5 for speeding on her way to the studio, driving "forty-three miles an hour in a twenty-five-mile zone on Cahuenga Avenue."

Margaret Sullavan had never previously worked with Wyler— but she had briefly encountered him a year and a half earlier: Wyler was running a print of Julien Duvivier's French film *Poilp de Carotte*, in a screening room at Universal, when Sullavan opened the door and looked in, thinking it was the screening room for the dailies of her debut film, *Only Yesterday*. Before *The Good Fairy* was finished, Sullavan would battle with her director...and marry him.

Decades later Wyler's script girl, Freda [Lerch] Rosenblatt, recalled to Wyler biographer Jan Herman that while Sullavan seemed "very cute and had a winsome sort of appeal, she didn't care what happened to anybody. She did spiteful things to get her way. If she was tired and wanted to go home and Willy had one more scene to do, she would smear the makeup on her face. That would mean everything had to stop so she could be made up again. Which might take hours. So they couldn't shoot." [Another time, she added] "Maggie got so bored between scenes she went behind one of the sets and purposely lay down on the dusty floor. The beautiful white dress she was wearing was a wreck. That stopped everything."

Wyler himself told writer Axel Madsen that he and Sullavan fought/disagreed so much that when watching dailies, he thought she looked so bad that *The Good Fairy* cinematographer Norbert Brodine wasn't photographing her well at all. Brodine defended himself by telling Wyler, "Each time you have a fight with her, she's unhappy and doesn't look good. When she's happy, she looks beautiful. You have a fight with her, she looks terrible." Wyler decided to make peace with Sullavan for the sake of the picture, and asked Sullavan to dinner. They went out a second time, and a third. Romance blossomed practically overnight and Wyler found he was absolutely crazy about her. The thought of marriage popped into this bachelor's head one evening while they were watching dailies of the picture's wedding scene. Unable to decide which takes were best, Wyler and Sullavan reviewed the scene together in the projection room–the same one where they'd briefly met 18 months earlier—long after the rest of the staff had gone home. Now he sat next to his leading lady in the dark, smoking a cigarette and watching her in the picture's final scene–the wedding. "Do you think," he whispered to her, "there is any law against a star marrying her director?" Sullavan leaned in, squeezed his arm and whispered: "I'll tell you tomorrow."

The nervous would-be bridegroom confided in Sturges who reassured him with, "Sure, why not." Sullavan arrived the next morning telling Wyler that "there is no law against an actress marrying her director. I looked it up." But how to tell his parents, Leopold and Melanie, who had recently arrived from Europe and always assumed he would find himself a nice Jewish girl? Wyler's father asked him, "What did you say her name was? Solomon?"

By the start of November, Herbert Marshall's scenes were complete. He was staying at the Beverly Hills Hotel and Bungalows while shooting retakes of *The Painted Veil* at M-G-M and took up a pencil to hand-write Wyler a letter on the hotel's stationery on November 8th:

My Dear Willy,

Re-takes at Metro prohibit me from coming out to Universal and telling you personally what a pleasant time I had with you— and I'm leaping off to the Desert to-morrow evening. I enjoyed myself enormously and I shall use my next drink into toasting you and wishing you and the company and Preston a successful picture, artistically and box-officially.

You might please tell Margaret, with my regard, that in spite of any view she may have to the contrary, her gum-chewing is nowhere near as good as her acting, and God knows her chewing is superb and adroit.

Yours sincerely,

Bart.

"[P.S.] Then, of course, up crops the question of the re-takes, and I'll tell you later how I shall have enjoyed <u>them</u>!"

Wyler and Sullavan chose to keep the upcoming wedding secret and fly to Yuma, Arizona, just across the state border, on a chartered DC-3, thus avoiding California's three-day waiting period. Freda Rosenblatt later recalled to author Jan Herman that there may have been another reason for the secrecy besides avoiding publicity: word of the wedding-to-be got out and Jed Harris showed up unexpectedly on the set and asked Sullavan to marry him. Wyler himself told Sullavan's daughter Brook Hayward that "I think trying to get away from Jed Harris contributed to the fact that she married me."

Wyler and Sullavan were wed in Yuma on Nov. 25, 1934 by the "marrying justice" Earl A. Freeman, who was clad in a bathrobe & slippers. Freeman's wife was in the bathroom & couldn't come out although she was the "witness" so the marriage certificate was slipped under the door for her to sign.

REGINALD OWEN: "Detlaff," the waiter.

A native Englishman and professional actor since the age of 18, John Reginald Owen never needed to wait tables in his life, nor was he a bachelor. In Hollywood for three years, he and Frank "Konrad" Morgan, who play each other's nemesis in *The Good Fairy*, were in "real life" the best of friends, socializing and enjoying games of bridge. A few months before filming began, "Reggie" celebrated his marriage to his second wife, a young divorced ex-showgirl named "Billey Edis" (her real name). Soon after their marriage, a *Los Angeles Times* item noted that a party at the home of Dimitri Tiomkin and Albertina Rasch, with guests including Edward G. Robinson, Patsy Ruth Miller, and Richard Boleslawsky, "... turned into a fete for Reginald Owen and his bride...Frank Morgan, arriving at 2 a.m. after working far into the night, found the affair just about to break up, but on his appearance it started up all over again." Reggie and Frank no doubt had a marvelous competitive time trying to outdo each other as Detlaff and Konrad.

JUNE CLAYWORTH: "Mitzi," the onscreen movie wife.

This svelte and stylish actress was every bit as elegant in real life as her brief onscreen character but not yet married. She was born Esther Cantor in New Jersey on June 5, 1905, to David and Ida

Schwartz Cantor who had immigrated to America in 1901. Carl Laemmle, Jr. saw her in the stage show *Are You Decent* and gave her a screen test in the summer of 1934.

GAVIN GORDON: "Meredith," the onscreen movie husband.

His full name was Fred Gavin Gordan, and he was a southern boy, born in Mississippi and raised in Alabama, living in Hollywood with his sister Lottie, 12 years his senior. Before becoming a stage actor, he was a stenographer for a railroad in Mobile Alabama.

CESAR ROMERO: "Joe," the "stage door Johnny."

Cesar Romero was under contract to Universal and had only appeared in a handful of films by the time he was chosen for this brief appearance in *The Good Fairy*, but he was no "bit" player. He'd just co-starred in Universal's comedy *Cheating Cheaters*, which was released in early November, opposite Fay Wray of *King Kong* fame. Romero knew Margaret Sullavan from when they were both "unknowns" in 1930 in the southern touring company of the Preston Sturges' comedy *Strictly Dishonorable*. Romero later recalled how Sullavan would talk to him of her boyfriend "Hank"–Henry Fonda.

ERIC BLORE: "Dr. Metz" the Minister of Arts and Decorations.

Like his onscreen character, the ever-tipsy Dr. Metz, Eric Blore had an over-fondness for the bottle. At the time of filming, this London-born actor had been in the United States since 1923 and was the father of a seven year old son, Eric Jr., with his second wife, American actress Clara Mackin. Blore's first wife, a beautiful English girl named Violet Winter, had died in early 1919 in London, after just one and a half years of marriage. He had served in World War I as a lieutenant in the South Wales Borderers and then put in charge of a division concert troupe. His first big Broadway stage success came with the Fred Astaire/Claire Luce musical *Gay Divorce* in 1932, which brought him to Hollywood in 1933. He recreated his small but memorable role as the waiter in RKO's Astaire/Ginger Rogers film version, entitled *The Gay Divorcee*.

FRANK MORGAN: "Konrad," owner of the South American Meat-Packing Company.

Frank Morgan, born Francis Phillip Wuppermann in New York City, was 44 years old, married for 20 years to the same woman, and the father of an 18-year-old son named George when he began work on *The Good Fairy*. An elder brother, Ralph, was in the movies too, as a contract player for Fox films and, a year earlier, the first president of a new actors union called Screen Actors Guild. It is evident when Morgan's "Konrad" enthuses to Lu that she makes him feel "forty...I mean twenty" that Konrad is supposed to be older than Frank himself. But, like Konrad, Frank had South American connections—his father, George Diogracia Wuppermann, was born in Angostura (now Ciudad Bolivar) Venezuela, as was Morgan's Spanish grandmother, Zoyla Gomez, born in Nutrias, Venezuela. The Wuppermann family wealth that enabled Frank to be raised in upper-middle class comforts originated in South America and was made in Trinidad: Dr. Siegert's Angostura Bitters.

By 1934, Morgan had been acting professionally for 20 years, since debuting in a significant romantic part in a short sketch entitled *The Last of the Quakers* opposite beautiful Hermine Shone in vaudeville, in January 1914, before secretly eloping with another beauty—teenage heiress Alma Muller. He did not begin his career as a "character" actor, but evolved into one by the late 1920s.

Had fate not cruelly intervened, there might have been a third "Morgan" brother in Hollywood in 1934 besides Ralph and Frank: "Carlyle Morgan," was an actor, poet and playwright who lost his life in Trier, Germany in the allied occupation period after World War I, in 1919. The Great War (as Word War I was initially called) had been over nearly 16 years before *The Good Fairy* filming began. While Frank Morgan did not fight in that great cataclysm, he bore scars from it through the loss of this elder brother, born Carlos Wuppermann, who died from a bullet through his head while in service with the Corps of Intelligence Police. As a result, Frank had become a high-functioning alcoholic, but never let liquor interfere with his performances: he was always letter-perfect in his lines. The war brought Morgan an additional loss: movie director and actor Sidney Rankin Drew, who directed and performed with him in his silent film debut, *The Suspect,* in 1916, had joined the Lafayette Flying Corps in France and was killed there in 1918.

The "Great War" also took something from Herbert Marshall, Frank's onscreen competitor for Margaret Sullavan—his right leg.

HERBERT MARSHALL: "Dr. Max Sporum."

Herbert "Bart" Marshall was the third Englishman in the cast and exactly nine days older than Frank Morgan. He was on his second marriage, to British actress Edna Best, and the father of a little girl, Anne (a future actress herself) who was currently in England with her mother. Marshall and Edna Best were estranged at the time and the newspapers politely commented on his squiring 'round town with glamorous actress Gloria Swanson—who had just sought a divorce from her most recent husband, Michael Farmer. Herbert Marshall was a Paramount contract player in great demand as a leading man and had just completed *The Painted Veil* at Metro-Goldwyn-Mayer with Greta Garbo when Universal won his services for *The Good Fairy.*

Edwin Schallert informed his *Los Angeles Times* readers on August 22nd that negotiations were underway for Marshall to be loaned out for *The Good Fairy* and that "even the newer and younger leading women, it is felt, need to have his proficient romanticism displayed in their pictures."

Like all the male actors of *The Good Fairy,* Marshall was a stage professional before war began in August 1914. Unlike many enthusiastic young Britons, however, Marshall did not volunteer for service. Conscription was introduced in Britain at the end of January 1916 covering all men between the ages of 18 and 41 who were unmarried or widowed as of November 2, 1915. Marshall was married and thus initially conscription-safe and as a stage actor can hardly be blamed for not wishing to join in the bloodshed. But, as British military losses increased, conscription was extended to married men on May 25, 1916. According to Marshall's war service record, he joined the 14th Battalion London Regiment, the "London Scottish" on June 2, 1916, mobilized Aug. 29, 1916 and was sent to France Jan. 4, 1917, disembarking the following day. His agonizing wound came on April 9, 1917, the same day that British poet

Edward Thomas was killed by a shell at the Battle of Arras. Marshall's service record notes it as simply "GSW [gun shot wound], knee" but not where his battalion was when it occurred. Marshall was sent home on May 2 and a year later, on May 17, 1918, discharged as "no longer physically fit for war service." His service record does not record when, or where, the amputation took place.

No young "leading men" of stage or screen at this time, was an amputee. Marshall refused to allow his painful handicap to deter him.

The Good Fairy's "Dr. Sporum" owed his ramrod straight and stiff walking gait to Herbert Marshall's artificial limb.

Marshall's condition was not generally written of in the mainstream Hollywood press of the time, but it was an "open secret." Whisperings of "Herbert Marshall has a wooden leg." This was of course was inaccurate—he had a prosthetic device, not something like Captain Ahab would have stumped around on. One little actress who heard the "wooden" leg rumor was twelve-year-old Jean Darling; formerly a starlet of Hal Roach's *Our Gang* comedies, she was determined to learn the truth. As she told interviewer Tony Villecco in *Silent Stars Speak*, she was going to St. Augustinian Church in Culver City—across the street from M-G-M where Marshall was filming *The Painted Veil*, with Garbo in 1934—and had an idea. She found Marshall on *The Painted Veil* set in a chair looking over his script, walked up and "accidentally" touched and tapped his knee. She repeated the "accident" on the other knee. Marshall informed the curious child, "It's the right one! Why didn't you *ask* which one?" The embarrassed little girl replied, "I didn't want to be rude."

Marshall's disability was also recalled by British playwright/director, and former actor, Reginald Denham, four years Marshall's junior, who acted with him in England after the war. In 1966 after Marshall died, Denham wrote to *Variety* painting a vivid word-picture of Marshall's stoic determination to overcome a handicap none of his fellow actors had to contend with. As he told it, he and Marshall were engaged for John Drinkwater's play *Abraham Lincoln* opening at the Lyric in Hammersmith, London in February 1919, just three months after the armistice brought the effective end to the "Great War." Denham recalled, "We had rehearsed for three weeks and it was not until the dress rehearsal when we were taking off our clothes that we discovered that 'Bart,' as we called him, had only one leg... Bart... had one of the latest mechanical ones for which there was a growing demand. These postwar contraptions were extremely clumsy and would cause the wearer great pain. Several years later Bart told me that he had played most of the run of *Lincoln* in agony." Compounding Marshall's challenges were three swift costume changes and a third floor dressing room, requiring him to go up and down the stairs eight times each day—double on matinee days. Denham marveled: "Through all this crippling discomfort I never heard Bart utter a word of complaint. Of course, we all tried to help him in his quick change when circumstances allowed. His one reaction, apart from gratitude, was apologetic. He hated being such a 'bloody nuisance.'"

Another time, Denham relayed, a young pre-war actor-manager friend of Marshall's visited the dressing room and "...suggested that, because of Bart's disability, he was fighting a losing game in trying to resume his acting career [and] advised him to try front-of-the-house desk work if he was still stage struck. Bart told this popinjay what to do with himself in terms that would have won the approval of Kenneth Tynan [famous British theatrical critic]."

A year later, in 1920, Denham appeared with Marshall again, in *The Merchant of Venice*—Marshall as Antonio and Denham in the small part of "Safanio—and "Bart" had an improved artificial leg. But challenges remained, as Denham described: "One day, without warning, he lost his balance and crashed to the floor in the middle of a scene. [The actor playing] Salarino and I helped him to his feet. He quickly regained composure and went on as if nothing unusual had happened. When the curtain fell his reaction was typical. He apologized to everybody for wrecking the scene and being a 'bloody nuisance.' In most of his obituary notices, he seems to be remembered as having been a superb exponent of elegant 'perfect gentleman' parts, which indeed he was. However, my own main memory of him is as a young eagle, a wounded eagle with indomitable courage."

All the *Good Fairy* cast members are gone–Frank Morgan was the first to pass away, in his sleep at the age premature of 59, on September

18, 1949, followed less than four months later by 57 year-old Alan Hale, who, as obituaries stated, died of a "liver infection complicated by a virus infection." Margaret Sullavan was the youngest to die, at age 50 in Connecticut on New Year's Day 1960 from a drug overdose that may, or may not have been intentional. The last survivor was dapper Cesar Romero dying in Santa Monica, California on New Year's Day of 1994, just 2 ½ weeks before Los Angeles' devastating Northridge earthquake. But their performances live on, thanks to the survival of the physical film itself, safety prints of which are often screened at revival houses and film festivals, combined with the magic of cable television, home video, video on demand and mobile media—inconceivable in 1935 and miraculous today.

The Shaggy D.A.
Anatomy of a Sequel

By Charles Tranberg

In 1959 Walt Disney Studios released *The Shaggy Dog*, a film that cost peanuts to produce and went on to gross more than $9 million at the box office, the third biggest-grossing film of the year. *The Shaggy Dog* was the first live-action comedy in the studio's history.

Its success helped define the studio's live-action output for the next twenty years. Increasingly Disney presented moderately budgeted slapstick comedies that featured an unexplainable situation to big box office rewards. These films included *The Absent-Minded Professor, Son of Flubber, The Misadventures of Merlin Jones, The Monkey's Uncle, Blackbeard's Ghost, The Love Bug, The Barefoot Executive, The Computer Wore Tennis Shoes* and *Million Dollar Duck*. It's interesting that while *The Absent-Minded Professor* was very nearly as successful as *The Shaggy Dog* and spanned a sequel (*Son of Flubber)* which was almost as successful as the original film—*The Shaggy Dog* didn't generate a sequel for nearly seventeen-years, until *The Shaggy D.A.* (1976). "I think it was felt that this was a good formula," Jan Williams, who began with the studio as a stand-in and later evolved into a producer later recalled, "and with Dean Jones, Suzanne Pleshette and Tim Conway it was a natural for an upgrade."

The Shaggy D.A. cast popular Disney star Dean Jones (he was to Disney Studios in the 1970's what Fred MacMurray was to it in the 1960's) as Wilby Daniels, the part played by Tommy Kirk in the original film. Set in the town of Medfield (the setting for five other Disney comedies—the *Flubber* films and the Kurt Russell "Dexter Riley" college trilogy), Wilby is now an adult who is happily married (and who wouldn't be if your wife is played by Suzanne Pleshette?) and a successful attorney. Wilby is running for District Attorney against the corrupt current DA (played by the always terrific Keenan Wynn). Of course complications arise when the ring that had turned him into a dog when he was a teenager is stolen from a museum and the inscription is read (*"In canis corpore transmute")* and Wilby again becomes the shaggy sheep dog he was in the original film. Naturally this gets very inconvenient for somebody who is campaigning for public office, constantly to turn into a sheepdog! Especially under the gleam of TV cameras. This was the Disney Studios' post-Watergate look at politics in the United States.

Chosen to direct *The Shaggy D.A.* was Disney legend, Robert Stevenson, the gentle Englishman who had directed nineteen Disney films since 1957, including *Mary Poppins* (he became at the time the only Disney director to be nominated for an Academy Award as Best Director), *Old Yeller, The Absent-Minded Professor,* and *The*

Love Bug—the highest grossing film of 1969. This would be Stevenson's last film. Dean Jones later recalled Stevenson fondly:

(Our director) Robert Stevenson—I think history will probably judge him as having been a very significant director if we just look in terms of the number of people who paid their bucks at the box office. He'd say, 'give me one more just like that' and I'd say, 'why don't you just print the one you got?' and he would always say with a sly smile, 'there was a technical problem.' (New Straits Times, 5/3/86)

Jan Williams also recalls Stevenson, "He had storyboards everywhere. He utilized storyboards more than any director I ever worked with… even dialogue scenes, he knew what words would be on camera from what actors. He cut the film in the camera. Very precise, exacting and with little patience. He would shoot a scene and like a machine gun say… cut… print… over here, and he was ready for the next shot."

Along with Dean Jones, Suzanne Pleshette and Keenan Wynn was the usual Disney stock company of fine character actors applying their trade in smaller (yet showy) roles which enlivened a number of Disney films of the era, including Jo Anne Worley, Dick Van Patten, Hans Conried, Vic Tayback, Hank Jones, Tim Conway, Michael McGreevey and Jonathan Daly. McGreevey, who plays Sheldon, candidly recalls the film (his final after more than a decade of service to the studio), "I think it was a film that was just a hodge-podge mixture of a lot of comedic formulas that had worked in previous Disney live-action films. But the film had no identity of its own; it had no original hook or storyline that would engage the audience. I felt it was a very episodic and disjointed movie that had no clear storyline for the audience to follow."

Hank Jones, another Disney veteran of more than a decade, recalls, "I played a frustrated cop trying to corral Dean, who then turned into the huge sheepdog. Suzanne Pleshette was also cast in the film and when I showed up to film a scene she greeted me with a 'Where's your track suit?' because the last time we had worked together had been when I was Gunder in *Blackbeard's Ghost* (1968, another Disney film). A major challenge in this movie was trying not to break up at the antics of Tim Conway, whom I was attempting to arrest in one of the closing scenes. Tim is a bit nuts and his

off-the-wall comic riffs make it near impossible to keep a straight face and stick to the script. Somehow I did—but it was tough!"

Peter Renaday (another perennial member of the Disney stock company) also recalls Conway, "I did one scene with Tim Conway in that picture and Stevenson (the director) thought I looked too young for the part (I was about 40), so the make-up people did what they could to age me up. I played a roller derby ticket player and Tim did some funny shtick getting his fingers caught in my pocket when he tried to put his ticket there, but it was cut out of the picture!" Jan Williams recalls that "Tim Conway was the best. What you see on camera is Tim Conway. I did a number of projects with Tim and never, NEVER could catch him in a serious moment. Dick Warlock, a stunt man on the picture, as well as several other Disney films, recalls Conway as "a fright! I can't say enough about his sense of humor on and off screen. What a blast to spend time with."

Dean Jones also was well-liked by the Disney stock company. "Dean was one of the top Disney leading men of the day and he was easy to work with and he followed Jimmy Cagney's sage advice about how to act: 'plant your feet firmly, look the other guy in the eye, and tell the truth,'" recalls Hank Jones. "He had a natural likability that came through in his performances." Jan Williams recalls Jones as, "A funny guy, a warm guy, a pro always willing to do another take without carping."

Suzanne Pleshette was popular with the cast and crew as well. She was well-known for her bawdy personality and the use of four letter words, but, like the similar Carole Lombard, she never lost her femininity. Actor Jonathan Daly, a veteran of seven Disney films and numerous other films and TV shows (including a season playing film legend James Stewart's son on *The Jimmy Stewart Show*) recalls Pleshette as, "fun and yet a total pro—a fantastic gal. Suz would bring me chicken or cheese every day at 4pm so that my energy would keep up." Hank Jones also has fond memories of Pleshette: "Suzanne Pleshette was films' leading lady and she was one of Hollywood's most genuinely liked performers. She was beautiful, sexy, and super-bright, says it like it is—and had the foulest mouth in town." Jan Williams echoes this, "Susanne Pleshette was a blast! With a mouth like a truck driver, but never offensive, only used for effect."

Another key member of *The Shaggy DA* cast was an English Sheep Dog named Ollie. Producer Bill Anderson spent weeks auditioning sheep dogs. How does a movie producer audition a sheep dog? "The same way I would interview any other actor," Anderson told columnist Bob Thomas, "I look for personality, appeal, how does the dog react? Does it cower? Or does it respond appealingly to every situation." And how did Ollie pass muster? "He was the largest, prettiest and best behaved of all the dogs," Anderson recalled. "Nothing bothered him. He was loving and he minded. Perfect!" This was not Anderson's first encounter with dogs at Disney. He had been with the studio since 1943 and was an associate producer on the Disney classic *Old Yeller*. One of the challenges for Anderson and the Disney creative department was teaching Ollie how to speak on camera. "In the original picture the dog only talked in a couple of scenes," recalled Anderson. "The way they did it was to shoot the dog in profile and have someone work his mouth with a finger. We thought of doing that with Ollie, but Art Vilarelli, who was going to direct the second unit stunts, said, 'That dog will bite your finger off.' Next we tried masks, and we got Bob Schiffer, who is the best in the business. But the masks didn't seem right.

Our director, Bob Stevenson, suggested cutting the dog talk, but I thought there must be some way to do it. Either the dog could be taught to 'speak'—by opening and closing his mouth—or he could chew." In the end they shot film of Ollie opening and closing his mouth–first at normal speeds and then they speeded it up and edited it into making it appear that Ollie (or Dean Jones as Ollie) is actually speaking.

The next trick was how to transform Dean Jones into Ollie, the sheep dog. According to Stevenson, "Dean was a great sport about it. Each stage of the transformation took two hours in makeup, and it took all day to shoot. Dean was not only patient about that, but he returned after the picture ended to record grunts, breathing and ad libs for the soundtrack. Those were important to bring the dog alive as a man—in half of the picture Dean is a dog!"

For the most part Ollie a dream to work with—except, like most actors, by the end of a long work day. One scene in the script called for Suzanne Pleshette to kiss Ollie goodbye, and as she was about to kiss him he began to growl. The director called cut. The next day Pleshette, usually a cooperative dream to work with, called Anderson and said, 'If that goddam dog bites me in the face I'm going to own Disney Studios!' Pleshette offered her own interpretation of the scene in question. "That was the first time I ever wanted a stand-in for a love scene," she told columnist Joan Crosby. "When I suggested the stand-in at the studio, I suggested the alternative. I asked them how they would like for me to own the studio and finish the film with a brown paper bag over my head—in case my co-star became aggressive."

When *The Shaggy D.A.* opened nationally in December, 1976 it received mixed reviews, but solid box office sales. It was the kind of film that the public at the time expected from Disney. It was safe, predictable—and fun. Roger Ebert in his review wrote, "The movie's not without its moments. One of them occurs in the dog pound, where Jones (as a dog) has been imprisoned with a canine supporting cast. They all talk like classic Warner Brother's gangsters and one is given to singing sad laments while the others dig tunnels to freedom. It's an original premise—a cross between a dog movie and a prison movie—and all we need is Pat O'Brien as the warden. Or dogcatcher."

Variety, the (so-called) bible of show business, called the film "brisk" (which at 91-minutes it certainly is) and lauded the cast. "Jones is a pleasant light comedian whose style is perfectly suited to the WASPish world of Disney. As his wife, Suzanne Pleshette has her first film role in five years, and her beauty and intelligence livens a part that might have been dull without her. Rounding out a large and able supporting cast are such people as Tim Conway, JoAnne Worley (in her film debut), Dick Van Patten, Hans Conreid, and in an unbilled cameo as a dogcatcher, the late Liam Dunn, who died before completing his part. Conway is particularly droll as a cloddish ice-cream salesman."

More than thirty years later the film is still fun. The only thing missing from this sequel are more references to the original picture, *The Shaggy Dog.* As I was watching it I was thinking, 'Wouldn't it have been fun to have asked Fred MacMurray to do a cameo as Wilby's dog-hating, now retired postman dad again?' Or have a cameo with Annette Funnicello as one of Wilby's old girlfriends, who could cause a bit of jealousy with the Suzanne Pleshette character? This, I think, would have paid homage to the original film while still presenting an original story. I wonder if Walt might have thought of that.

The End

by Nat Segaloff

Death is a laughing matter to Sonny Lawson (BURT REYNOLDS) and his pal Marlon (DOM DE LUISE) in the outrageous comedy, "The End," a United Artists release.

Copyright © 1978. United Artists Corporation, all rights reserved. Printed in U.S.A.　　　TE-1

Anyone who says that nothing in life is certain but death and taxes never ran a film company. In Hollywood just the opposite is true: Movies about taxes are pretty much confined to how Elliott Ness nailed Al Capone, and death—even though it's a time-tested plot device—is egenerally limited to climaxes, not whole pictures.

Especially not comedies.

Jerry Belson thought otherwise. A successful television writer (*The Dick Van Dyke Show, The Odd Couple, The Mary Tyler Moore Show*, etc.), he was vacationing in Europe in 1971 when he read about a man who lay in a coma for eleven years before dying, despite having left specific termination instructions, when the hospital contravened his and his family's wishes in order to exploit his health insurance coverage. The serious yet insane situation struck Belson as the stuff of humor, and he spent the next nine months writing a script he called simply *The End*.[1]

"It was one of the greatest black comedies ever written," enthused James L. Brooks (*Terms of Endearment, The Simpsons*) years later. "We passed it around like religious papers. It was so funny and hard hitting."[2]

But despite his hot TV track record, Belson had no luck finding a movie buyer. "It went unfilmed for six years," he lamented. "Everyone said that it was funny but that they couldn't gamble on such a delicate subject matter.[3] Everybody who *couldn't* give me financing loved it; everybody who *could* hated it. After a couple of years I began to believe the haters."[4]

Eventually it landed on the desk of Burt Reynolds, who had just made his directorial debut with the action picture *Gator* in 1976 and was looking for something that could dignify his image. Since breaking out of television when his *Dan August* series folded in 1971, the likable Reynolds had bifurcated his career between playing good ol' boys in roughhouse pictures like *The Longest Yard* and *White Lightning* and hunky but approachable leads in *At Long Last Love* and *Lucky Lady*.

Reynolds' screen image has as many twists as one of his famous car chases. Although his heart originally lay in drama, he tarnished his Oscar® chances for his powerhouse performance in *Deliverance* (1972) by posing for a semi-nude centerfold in *Cosmopolitan* magazine within months of the film's release. How could anyone take him seriously after that? many felt. Yet it was this very ability to be both redneck and ribald that would endear him to a vast audience and make him the world's top screen star for ten years, five of them consecutive.[5]

---

1 Belson, Jerry, "I Wake Up Screening," *Los Angeles Times* column, May 7, 1978. Belson himself died on October 10, 2006 of cancer.

2 Quoted, McLellan, Dennis, "Comedy Writer Set the Standard," *Los Angeles Times*, October 13, 2006

3 Program notes, 1978 Los Angeles International Film Festival (FILMEX)

4 Belson, op cit

5 National Association of Theater Owners (1978–82)

But that wouldn't happen for a while; in 1976 *The End* still couldn't get a budget with Reynolds attached. It would be more than a year before the filmmakers found the money. What happened wasn't that *The End* was suddenly deemed commercial. Rather, Burt Reynolds was.

The reason was *Smokey and the Bandit.*

The action-adventure-car-truck-beer movie opened in May of 1977, the same month as *Star Wars,* and attracted everyone who wasn't going to a galaxy far, far away as well as millions who were. Over $55 million in rentals later (that's money flowing to the company, not raw theatrical gross), Burt Reynolds could, as he put it, have played a banana and they would have let him. Instead, he wanted to play a dying man.

Still, recalled Belson, "Everybody took pay cuts." Finally, United Artists stepped forward (not, surprisingly, Universal, which had *Smokey*). When *The End* was about to roll, added Belson, "They [UA] only had one little request: Could we please change the title from *The End* to *Smokey and the Bandit Gets Sick*"?[1]

Newly minted superstar Reynolds was equally glib when he spoke to the *New York Times'* Guy Flatley just before *The End* went into production. "This will be a big departure for me," he said. "I won't drive my car over 35 miles an hour and I won't take off my shirt. It's very easy for me to make little boy films where I chase sheriffs and cops and run them off the Alabama roads. I do that as well as anyone around, but I would like to grow as an actor. I haven't taken a chance in a long time, partly because the scripts that land on my desk are not exactly Al Pacino scripts."[2]

In point of fact, *The End* wasn't a "Burt Reynolds" script, either. According to legend, Belson wrote it with Woody Allen in mind even though, at the time, the highly selective Allen had acted in only one picture that wasn't made from his own material: *The Front* (1976) by Walter Bernstein. At first glance it would certainly seem that *The End's* main character would be more appropriate for someone with Allen's nebbishy image. Flatley disagreed, approving Reynolds' choice by venturing, "Mr. Reynolds, a man tragically

1 Belson, ibid
2 Flatley, Guy, *New York Times,* June 6, 1977

cursed with movie star charisma, has emphatic ideas about the sort of actor who would have been ideal as the hilariously doomed hero of *The End*."[1]

"I would go against the grain," Reynolds continued, "and try not to cast the obvious person: Woody Allen or Dustin Hoffman. I'd pick a leading man who had...machismo, but someone who could also do comedy. It's hard to find an actor like that...there just aren't many of them around."[2] Nor were there many scripts as edgy (before that word became its own satire) as *The End*, which remains one of Hollywood's miniscule number of black comedies. By convention, a "black comedy" has the ability to wring laughs out of things that are discomfiting to discuss, or even to think about. Unlike comic relief, which is often used to release a little steam from a heavy drama, in a black comedy the grotesquery itself is the basis for laughs. It's not just whistling while walking past the cemetery, it's making fun of how the bodies got there.

Technically, *The End* fits also loosely into the genre of a road picture in which the main character, Wendell Sonny Lawson (Burt Reynolds)[3], embarks on a quest and is helped along by a succession of disparate people, each of whom contributes to his ultimate enlightenment.

Its trajectory is relentless starting even before we fade up on a close-up of Reynolds' face pressed against an aquarium as he gets the bad news: Sonny, 39 (Reynolds was then 41), learns from his doctor (Norman Fell) that he will die of a toxic blood disease. Bursting into tears, he stumbles from the office and descends into self-pity. First he interrupts a funeral procession to ask the grieving widow what caused her husband's death (in return, she flips him off). Then he stuns a young priest (Robby Benson) by confessing sins that the newly minted padre can't handle. Finally he decides to commit suicide and ventures forth to bid farewell to (and wring

---

1 There is also talk that Paul Newman nursed the script but was unable to get backing, a prospect that seems unlikely given that the star was coming off *The Sting*, *The Towering Inferno*, and *The Drowning Pool*.

2 ibid

3 Reynolds' character's original name was "Sonny Williams" but a prominent note on the shooting script warns that it had to be changed to "Wendell Sonny Lawson" for legal reasons and that all the other Williamses should now be called Lawsons.

Egged on by Marlon (DOM DE LUISE), his best friend and worst enemy, Sonny Lawson (BURT REYNOLDS) prepares to take a plunge in "The End," a United Artists release.

TE-12

a little sympathy from) the people closest to him: his dispassionate parents (Myrna Loy and Pat O'Brien), his self-absorbed ex-wife Jessica (Joanne Woodward), his slovenly girlfriend Mary Ellen (Sally Field), his distracted lawyer Marty (David Steinberg) and, especially, his beloved teenage daughter Julie (Kristy McNichol). Each treats him in a manner that reflects the way he has presumably treated them: his parents take him for granted, Jessica detests him and won't listen, and Mary Ellen allows him to bed her, but it's mechanical. It is only teenage Julie who shows compassion and, in the end, it is she who inspires him to live. Well, as long as he can.

Meanwhile, Sonny discovers that suicide is easier threatened than committed. Using sleeping pills that he scarfs from his parents' well-stocked medicine cabinet ("So *that's* how they could stand to stay together all these years," he marvels), Sonny goes home, washes down the multi-colored meds with sour milk, and barfs them onto his glass coffee table ("It's like Walt Disney threw up," he groans). He passes out while remembering to write a farewell note to Julie and somehow awakens in a psychiatric hospital run by the ineffectual Dr.

Waldo Kling (Strother Martin).[1] There he is immediately befriended by Marlon Borunki (Dom DeLuise), a paranoid-schizophrenic who is murderously hung up on being Polish. Sonny and Marlon form a testy alliance and have adventures together in and out of the hospital, some of which involve Sonny's repeated attempts to kill himself and Marlon's continual comic outbursts trying to help him. When hanging, jumping, crushing, car chases, and bullets don't work, Sonny swims out to sea to drown. Only then does he realize that his daughter Julie makes his life worth living, and he unrepentantly bargains with God to carry him back to shore—where Marlon is armed and waiting.[2]

The worst thing a comedy can do is try to be funny, notes *The End*'s editor, Donn Cambern. "The idea was to make the characters real dramatically within the film," says Cambern, who has cut classics from *Easy Rider* to *Blume in Love* and *The Last Picture Show* to *Twins*. "That's how the comedy would emerge. We weren't making a 'comedy,' we were making a film where the comedy would emerge, like Woody Allen's or Paul Mazursky's films. They're full of laughs but their characters are so real in their own special world that that's where the comedy comes from."[3]

Few filmmakers, whether writers, directors, or hyphenates, can ride the balance between comedy and tragedy; most slip and fall off the fence. Billy Wilder (*Buddy Buddy*), Blake Edwards (*That's Life*), Alfred Hitchcock (*The Trouble with Harry*), James Whale (*The Old Dark House*), and Sidney Lumet (*Bye Bye Braverman*) succeeded to varying degrees, even if it took the public years to appreciate their skill. The only one whom everybody agrees hit the mark right off the bat was Stanley Kubrick with *Dr. Strangelove* and, to some extent, *Lolita.*

The End ups the ante, not merely by mentioning death but by dwelling on it, and not just death itself but suicide.

---

1 The script provides the connective tissue with a cut scene: he is discovered by two police who ticketed him for his funeral procession shenanigans.

2 Two endings were shot: one in which Marlon whips out a knife to stab the beached Sonny, ending in an indeterminate freeze frame; and a more slapstick one in which Marlon zig-zags along the beach chasing Sonny. The second, which played more hopeful, was used.

3 Cambern in interview with author, May 10, 2011

Some religions view suicide as a mortal sin, others as a release, and others as martyrdom. Few consider it commercial. Yet that's what United Artists decided when they announced the project five days after *Smokey and the Bandit*'s smash opening.[1] A week later Reynolds and producer Lawrence Gordon checked into the Goldwyn Studios (now Warner Bros.' The Lot) on Santa Monica Boulevard in Hollywood to begin casting and pre-production.[2] In short order they would attract Sally Field, Joanne Woodward, Pat O'Brien, Myrna Loy, Robby Benson, Carl Reiner, David Steinberg, and Dom DeLuise.

Principal photography began on July 11 in Los Angeles before moving to scenic Santa Barbara. As *The End* began, however, there was another drama in the works.

For decades United Artists' management had been among the most stable in the motion picture industry. The executive team of Arthur Krim, Robert Benjamin, Bill Bernstein, Mike Medavoy, and Eric Pleskow had enjoyed years of unparalleled success, both commercially and critically, since Krim and Benjamin acquired the floundering company from its surviving founders Mary Pickford and Charles Chaplin in 1950[3]. A sale to the San Francisco-based insurance conglomerate TransAmerica in 1968 assured them of financial security in a changing marketplace. Yet along with TransAmerica's dollars came TransAmeica's meddling as the bean counters tried to take over the most filmmaker-friendly company in the business. The 1970s saw a series of high level skirmishes between UA and TA. In 1977 Krim implored TA's chief, John Beckett, to spin off UA as a separate entity in which TA would retain a controlling interest but no controlling influence. Beckett refused. In January of 1978 Krim told *Fortune* magazine's Peter Schuyten, "You will not find any top officer here who feels that TransAmerica has contributed anything to United Artists."[4] In response, Beckett

---

1 "Smokey" opened May 19, 1977 and UA announced *The End* on May 24, 1977

2 *Box Office* magazine, June 6, 1977

3 Bergen, Ronald, *The United Artists Story*, NY: Crown Publishers, 1986. Page 87

4 quoted in Stephen Bach, *Final Cut*, NY: William Morrow and Company, 1985. Pages 56-57.

told Krim *et al* to love it or leave it. By the end of the month they had done the latter.

The Krim contingent quickly formed Orion Pictures and established a relationship with Warner Bros. to distribute their forthcoming product. Those on their former management team who remained at UA, such as executives James Harvey, Andy Albeck and Hy Smith, scrambled to back a blockbuster that would re-establish the bruised reputation of the orphaned company. They chose *Heaven's Gate*, but that's another story.

Meanwhile, almost lost in the shuffle was *The End*.

If comedy is drama plus distance, black comedy is drama so over the top that you cringe and laugh at the same time. But it is nervous laughter and needs to be focused. In *The End*, this task falls to actor-director Reynolds who forsakes his own star status to encourage comic performances from others. It was a huge gamble. Like Cary Grant, Reynolds' sex appeal grew stronger the more he denied it, and his ingratiating self-mocking made him his era's most skillful and engaging farceur. In *The End* he swings between deadpan and desperate, depending on whom he's playing against in any given scene. With Fell's chilly doctor, for instance, he crumbles in tears; with Woodward's fiery ex-wife, he's stoic; with Benson's Bambi-like priest, he's self-conscious. Sometimes it works, sometimes it doesn't, but there was no instruction booklet that came with Belson's script, so the fact that it got to the screen at all is remarkable.

But not all of it made it in. One early scene that was shot but fell by the wayside was a cameo by veteran actor Sam Jaffe (the High Lama in Frank Capra's 1937 *Lost Horizon*) playing a terminally ill hospital patient from whom Sonny asks the meaning of life and death, since he looked closer to the latter than the former. In the script (scene 21-23) the old man comes off as comically bitter. On the screen, not so much.

"It was a good scene," says executive producer Hank Moonjean (who went on to do many more films with Reynolds), "but it was so real we thought he was gonna die right there on the set."[1] A few other moments were trimmed, too, such as a moment with an unctuous insurance man who presses Sonny for a pre-death settlement,

---

1 Moonjean interview with the author, April 11, 2011. Jaffe died on March 24, 1984.

and a lunatic who is absolutely obsessed with the word *absolutely*. By and large, however, what was shot went into the finished 100-minute movie.

Comparing the results to its various script rewrites (July 6, 13, and 26; and August 11 and 13) one sees a gradual pulling back from Belson's outrageousness. Profanity is dropped and Sonny's comments become more benign. Perhaps in rehearsal the filmmakers grew cautious; perhaps movie stars just want to be loved; perhaps it just felt wrong when said out loud. But whatever the film loses in spleen, it gains in heart. The turning point occurs halfway through the picture when Sonny meets the man who will change not only his character's odyssey but that of Burt Reynolds' personal life as well: Dom DeLuise.

DeLuise and Reynolds had met by coincidence (or Fate) five years earlier when they were both guests on "The Tonight Show starring Johnny Carson." It was shortly after Reynolds' playful *Cosmo* centerfold and DeLuise honored it with his interpretation, set to Strauss's prologue to *Also Sprach Zarathustra*,[1] of what Burt Reynolds is like getting up in the morning. Dom stretched, preened, plumped, preened some more, and finally strutted over to Johnny. By then Carson, the audience, and, more importantly, Reynolds, were in stitches. The day after (September 16), Reynolds dispatched a note[2] to DeLuise's home that said, "Dear Dom, would you please leave me alone? Love, Burt." From that, a friendship developed that spanned six more films and countless TV shows, ending only with DeLuise's death on May 4, 2009.

"He's right there," DeLuise once said of Reynolds. "He's like the brother that cares for you."[3] For his part, Reynolds said of DeLuise, "Dom always made you feel better when he was around, and there will never be another like him."[4]

DeLuise and Reynolds had worked together only once before *The End*—a brief shower scene in Mel Brooks' 1976 comedy *Silent Movie*—and their chemistry was instantaneous. Reynolds' baffled

---

1 A.K.A. "the theme from '2001: A Space Odyssey.'"
2 Letter from Reynolds, Dom DeLuise Special Collection, Academy of Motion Picture Arts and Sciences
3 Comments to author
4 AP report, May 5, 2009

expressions at DeLuise's inventiveness in *The End* madness make both of them shine. In fact, of all the performers in *The End*, only DeLuise, whose sense of spontaneity was legendary on and off the screen,[1] was allowed to depart from Belson's script.

"When he came on he was catalytic," Cambern recalls. "He was hysterical. I used to come over and watch them shoot, as well. I just loved to be on the [stage] floor."

DeLuise's most notable addition came when he saw the script notation "to self" in his monologue in scene 55 in which Sonny wakes up in the mental hospital. Suddenly DeLuise began arguing with himself as a dual personality, leaving a baffled Reynolds out of the exchange, and it was so effective that Belson eagerly adapted the part to showcase the ebullient comic actor.

When he wrapped for the day, however, DeLuise felt that he had not done the scene justice. It was his first day on the picture after returning from a two-week European vacation with his wife, Carol, who had cued him on his lines as they crossed the Atlantic on the Queen Elizabeth II. Reynolds' speedy shooting pace with his all-important character introduction left DeLuise cold, and he offered to finance a re-shoot out of his own pocket. Reynolds declined, assuring the uncertain comic actor that it would all work out in the end.[2]

Directing only his second picture, Reynolds was in the company of what would become, over the years, his continuing support cadre.

"The crew loved him," Hank Moonjean recalls, and offers an example of the star's dry humor. "A generous man. He used to go around saying, 'I got the worst makeup man in Hollywood.' I said, 'What do you want him for?' and he said, 'I feel sorry for him.'"

He surrounded himself with partisans from earlier films: longtime stunt coordinator Hal Needham (whose *Smokey* had just taken off), actor-buddy James Best, cinematographer Bobby Byrne (*Smokey*, *Nickelodeon*), costume designer Norman Salling (*Nickelodeon*, *Gator*, *Hustle*), makeup artist Tom Ellingwood (everything since *Fuzz*), and his then-sweetheart Sally Field.

---

1 Mel Brooks often noted that he had to add two days to the schedule of any film that DeLuise was in because everybody laughed so much.

2 Author's conversation with Carol DeLuise.

According to reports, Reynolds ran a loose but efficient set despite the pressures of being both star and director. He seldom went more than two takes on any set-up unless there was a technical glitch such as someone slipping out of the shot or an airplane flying overhead.[1] He boldly covered several scenes in unbroken master shots, relying on the timing of seasoned pros like Field and Woodward to pace the comedy. He even urged his crew to make contributions, and one of them came up with Marlon's shouted warning as he and Sonny escape from the sanitarium: "That man's nuts; grab 'em!" For weeks after the film's release, young viewers took glee repeating it in public.[2]

Reynolds let scenes play out, but he also knew when to break them up with coverage (multiple angles) so editor Donn Cambern could hone the comic timing. To this end, for example, there is a script note on the Reynolds-Benson scene that says, "Intercut this sequence between Sonny and Priest, or not, when the line is funnier off stage." In other words, we'll fix it in Post.

"Burt had a very clear idea," Cambern reports, "and it was interesting because he did not look at dailies; I would look at dailies by myself. [Producer] Larry [Gordon] once in a while would look at dailies; Jerry [Belson] maybe once in a while, but not much; and I was just putting the film together. It was wonderful, truly wonderful. It was absolutely clear to me how scenes would cut together, it was so well directed and so funny."

Production went so well that principal photography wrapped under budget and two days ahead of schedule on March 28, 1977 before moving into a smooth post-production.

Unusual for a comedy, there weren't any studio sneak previews—Directors Guild-mandated test screenings so the filmmakers can tweak their work before the studio has a turn.

"We had a screening at Goldwyn," Cambern reports, "and Burt invited Mel Brooks and a whole audience there. Dom was there. Larry was there, of course. All for that purpose: how was this film really playing? We had practically nothing to do after that. It was practically on its feet."

---

1 September 21, 1977 cutting script prepared by script supervisor Kathy Thomas.
2 Author's conversation with Michael DeLuise.

Other than the decision to remove the Sam Jaffe scene, which was made prior to the screenings, *The End* went out as-is. But not without a speed bump. The Motion Picture Association of America gave the film an "R" rating for its theme and foul language despite the filmmakers' removal of several swear words in the looping process.

Reviewers were generally trifurcated in their appraisals: Some found its comedy forced, others liked it but found that its energy slacked as it went on; others appreciated Reynolds' skill in blending comedy and drama with frequent moments of genuine sentiment.

In a sense, all three were correct. Belson's original screenplay is shamelessly, gloriously, cathartically offensive. Reflecting the what-have-I-got-to-lose mindset of its dying protagonist, the original 124-page shooting script dated June 29, 1977 is full of things you'd love to say if you didn't care what people thought about you after you were gone. Sonny Lawson is, after all, a crooked real estate mogul at whom Fate is flipping its middle finger. But movie stars don't play heels, at least not for an entire picture, and, as Sonny softens, so does the movie. At the same time, *The End* sails into uncharted comic waters (certainly for a studio film; indie filmmakers John Waters and Robert Downey, Sr., had been swimming there for years).

For their part, the U.S. Catholic Conference condemned the picture, finding it to be a "painfully unfunny" comedy that is "seriously offensive in its disrespectful treatment of confession and an explicit scene of lovemaking."[1]

The Polish community took the picture personally. Three lawsuits were launched against the film, Burt Reynolds Productions, and United Artists by Polish-American groups who took offense at the litany of Polish jokes fired by the self-hating Marlon Borunki, a fusillade made perversely effective by DeLuise's comic marksmanship. The first legal action came from Thomas Czerwinski, president of the 15,000-member local chapter of the Polish American Congress in Milwaukee, Wisconsin. Czerwinski wanted all advertising for *The End* to carry a prominent warning that some persons might find it offensive. "They advertise it as funny," he told the *Los Angeles Times*. "We say it is not funny, especially to Polish Americans. If it

---

1 *Weekly Variety*, May 1, 1978

was black or Jewish humor it wouldn't be funny, and Burt Reynolds wouldn't even think about it. This will be a landmark case." Saying he would sue under the state's consumer protection laws, he added, "We hope to create a prototype of a means to defend ourselves against this time of sub-human stereotyping against Polish-American kids."[1] There is no record of the disposition of the case.

Chicago resident Leonard Jarczab, self-described as the head of the Polish American Guardian Society, demanded $1 million in his lawsuit for libeling his people as "depraved, filthy, lewd, unpatriotic, stupid, the equivalent of human excrement and totally lacking in any virtue or redeeming qualities." His action was dismissed as meritless in July of 1981 by Cook County, Illinois circuit judge Warren D. Wolfson who agreed that the material may indeed have been in bad taste but it was not libelous.[2] The following year a Massachusetts appellate court rejected a similar suit brought by the Polish-American Guardian Society that claimed not only libel but emotional distress. In its ruling, the Bay State Court held that a defamatory remark must be directed at someone specific and not merely at an indeterminate class of people[3]. Finally, *The End* was picketed at a theatre in Amsterdam, New York by town Mayor John Gomulka and 35 members of the local Polonaise society, none of whom admitted to having seen it. The demonstration took place ignominiously at a second-run house months after the film had closed its first-run openings[4].

But by then *The End* had become a hit. According to an MGM accounting (MGM acquired UA in 1982 after the latter's *Heaven's Gate* debacle drove it into bankruptcy), by the end of 2000 *The End* showed a gross of slightly under $37,600,000 yielding net receipts—the figure against which everybody's profit participation would be computed—of almost $18 million.[5]

Much has changed in movie comedy since *The End*. Screen humor is more brutal now, even nihilistic. Additionally, except for Sonny's daughter, played by then-15-year-old Kristy McNichol,

---

1 *Los Angeles Times*, July 10, 1978

2 Los Angeles Times, July 11, 1981

3 *Hollywood Reporter*, March 20, 1981

4 *Weekly Variety*, November 8, 1978

5 MGM profit participation statement, DeLuise collection, AMPAS

The End is populated entirely by adults. Were it made today (fat chance) it would have to star twenty-somethings and appeal to teen audiences, few of whom would have knowledge of the kind of real-world emotions that Belson, Reynolds, *et al* are tweaking. In a way, it has become a kind of time capsule not only for its craft and performances but for a brand of artistic bravery that few major motion pictures today attempt, and at which even fewer have so audaciously succeeded.

Acknowledgments:

The Margaret Herrick Library: Linda Harris Mehr, Howard Prouty, Jenny Romero, Barbara Hall; Elizabeth Adams; Carol DeLuise; Michael DeLuise; Hank Moonjean; Donn Cambern

The North Avenue Irregulars
by Mike White

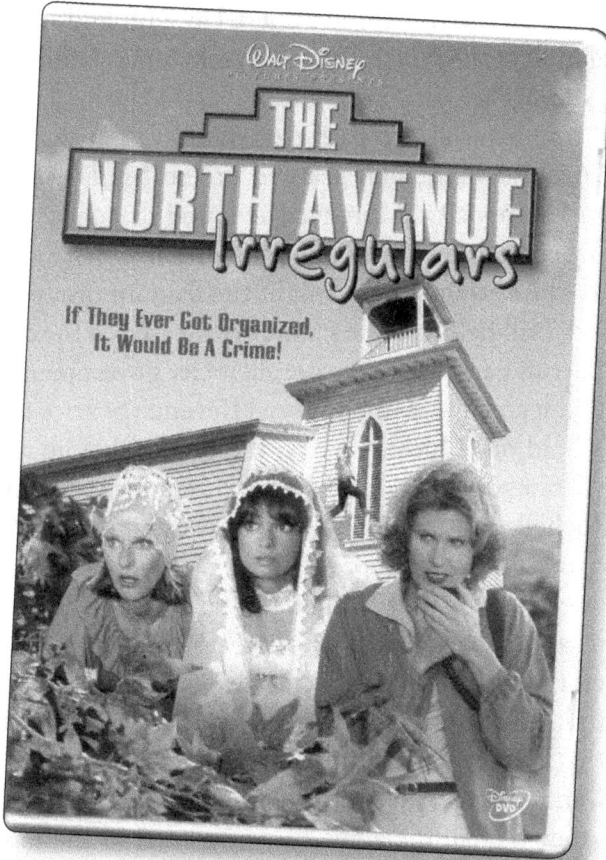

"People who wink at wrong cause trouble, but a bold reproof promotes peace."

– Proverbs 10:10 (New Living Translation)

Over the 60 years and 160 films of the Buena Vista distribution company's roster, only a handful were based on real life events. This arm of the Walt Disney Company became known for their live action comedies like *The Apple Dumpling Gang* (1975), *The Shaggy D.A.* (1976), and *Herbie Goes Bananas* (1980). Thus, it would be a natural assumption that the outrageous "Church versus Organized Crime" film, *The North Avenue Irregulars* (1978), ranked among the fictional entries Buena Vista released. Surprisingly, the events of the film, however loose the adaptation, stem from the true-life adventures of Reverend Albert Fay Hill and members of his congregation at the North Avenue Presbyterian Church in New Rochelle, New York.

Rev. Hill took over as the pastor of the North Avenue Church in early 1962, and he quickly learned of the Mafia's presence in Westchester County city. Moreover, he found that the city officials of New Rochelle not only condoned the illegal activity but openly discouraged Hill's attempt to spotlight the flagrant disregard to the law. By 1964, Hill held specific services dedicated to the discussion of the Mafia-run gambling and complicit city government.

Finally, Hill teamed with the Internal Revenue Service to bust up the Mafia's hold on "Queen City on the Sound" before he moved to Denver, Colorado to take over a new church pastorship. Hill left New Rochelle in July of 1968 and Cowles published *The North Avenue Irregulars* in October of that year.

Nearly a decade later, Roy Miller, the head of Buena Vista (and also son-in-law to Walt Disney), put *North Avenue Irregulars* on screen. Actor Edward Herrmann recalls, "It was still very much a family run place. I think that was the first year, very shortly after or before, that Disney Enterprise, the whole Disney mega-business broke even, and the stockholders were not pleased, because they had Epcot and they had all the amusement parks. And the movie side of things just wasn't producing the way they wanted it to produce."

Miller paired two of the stronger talents at Buena Vista, writer Don Tait (who penned all of the aforementioned films) and director Bruce Bilson. Oddly, the craze sweeping the nation, CB Radios, helped the film come to fruition.

Bruce Bilson recalls, "This was the time of CB radios, you know, 'What's your handle?' 'Over and out,' all that stuff. *Smokey and the Bandit*, and so on. The biggest part of the original script was to take advantage of that CB radio stuff and I never read the book *North*

Avenue, but it was put that together and make it, all these ladies on the radio. That was the script and we started working on it. I can't remember what we did, but I know what happened, Don [Tait] and Tom Leetch who was producer, we would meet on weekends in my condo. I was recently divorced and living there.

"We'd talk about where the script was going and Don would go home and write it. Then, the next week, we'd work on that and go on. That's how the script evolved. The rewrites, that's how the rewrites evolved. I'm not trying to take any credit away from anybody, we just worked together and came up with the script."

Don Tait adds, "[Bruce] made some contributions [...] like in the demolition derby towards the end there, things you don't put down on paper, visualize, and the director takes off on that sort of stuff. He did a good job. I wish he'd directed some of my other things."

After a stunning credit sequence from Disney animator Arthur "Art" Stevens and

Joe Hale (the two had worked together on *The Rescuers* and *The Fox & The Hound*) with a Henry Mancini-esque soundtrack from Robert F. Brunner (*Snowball Express*), the film opens on the North Avenue Presbyterian Church where a large portion of the events take place. This wild initial sequence has Mr. Rafferty (Douglas Fowley) being accidentally knocked out of the church belfry by Reverend HIll's two children. This scene of physical comedy shows how the parishioners (almost all portrayed as middle-aged women with spouses we don't see) can come together for common causes - cleaning and painting the church as well as saving Mr. Rafferty's life.

Regarding the church itself, Bruce Bilson says, "We had a big problem with the church that we were going to burn down and hang a guy off the roof, and all that stuff. The location guy [Howard ‹Dutch› Horton] went out and he kept bringing pictures of churches and we'd say, 'No, it doesn't have a steeple. No... how can you...' That went on. He'd go out and every couple weeks bring us more pictures. Then, one day, John Mansbridge, who was the head of the art department, came in with the drawing and he said, 'What would you think of this?'

"I said, 'Wow, that's terrific! Where is it?' We went out on the back lot and there was this southern mansion. He said, 'We're going to pick this up, turn it sideways, lengthwise. Then we'll put a steeple up on the top of it, with a little building sticking out for the school and office.'

"And that's what they did. They made that church on the back lot.

"The interior we shot at a church that's between my house and the studio. It's a neighborhood church in North Hollywood that is friendly to movie studios. We shot the interior there. The other big, big, big thing was the opening physical action sequence. That was another new experience for me.

"They have a graphic artist that does a frame-by-frame storyboard. He and I started working together and he was very clever. We worked out that whole sequence, beat-by-beat, then the dialogue was added and so on. There were these huge rolling blackboards like what they'd bring out in a schoolroom or something, but it was a pin board and we'd pin up all these pictures. Then we went to production and got to decide what piece of set we needed for each beat of that. So, if you look at it again, there was the top of the steeple itself as a separate unit where you could ring the bell and all that. Eventually the ladies got up there and the ladder went in and out and that was the biggest piece. So, you know there was a piece of it on the rope going up and down and that was on the stage with a piece of the side built. Then the inside was built, where the ladies went—that was not an accident that the ladder broke through the wall trying to get up the steps.

"Every beat of that there were six or seven pieces of set to make that work—some against the blue sky and such. We worked on that, little bits and pieces were put all over the schedule whenever they were built and they were on the stage and that had to be removed and some other piece brought it... that was a very big deal."

Another change from the book to the script was Albert Hill's name. Rechristened as "Michael Hill," this was an early film role for Edward Herrmann who is best known for either playing Franklin Delano Roosevelt in a number of films or for being the head vampire in *The Lost Boys* (1987). "I did four movies—big ones—*The Paper Chase*, *The Day of the Dolphin*, *The Great Gatsby*, and *The Great Waldo Pepper*. Those were all cast out of New York. I was still living in New York. I was brought out to do "Eleanor and Franklin" with Daniel Petrie directing. And this was shortly after that."

Herrmann continues, "I remember going in to read for a voice audition for *The Fox and the Hound*. There were guys in there, old men who were old to me at the time, that were directing me and giving me line readings and all of this. Coming from the theatre, the idea of giving me a line reading was just appalling. But they were the guys who did *Dumbo* and *Snow White*. So, keep your mouth shut, Hermann and listen to them.

"And they were so kind, they were so sweet. They had a sound stage there they tricked out for recording. That they'd build and developed to record the picture, and I passed this odd little hallway and in there was a wall made out of 2x4s covered in screens so you could see through. Just a bunch of shelves. And on those shelves was what looked like junk, egg beaters, whistles, pieces of iron, glass, crockery—God knows what. And I had a very fun time reading for these guys and we were talking about the movie business, and I was a young face out there. I asked what that room was, with all those objects on the shelves. They got quiet, and they said, 'Well, so-and-so just died and he was the key sound effects man for Mr. Disney—for Walt—for fifty years. And every one of those objects made a particular sound that was used from the '30s on into the '50s, '60s, '70s and he was the only one who knew what every single one of them did. He never labeled them, he just knew where to go to get the pops and the dings and the bings or the screeches—whatever you needed, he could find. All of those objects in there, no one had ever catalogued it, he hadn't written them down.' They were sort of lamenting that nobody there knew what half of them did. But that's how present Walt was at the studio while I was there.

"I was always coming from serious theatre and had played some heavyweight stuff. Especially after Roosevelt, I wanted the story to have a dangerous edge to it, because they were doing some dangerous things, but it was part of the Disney ethos to lighten it and make it children friendly. So life is never too dangerous. Never too dark. And that rankled, but that was the style of the studio. You couldn't break that, that was what Disney did. In a way, now, in retrospect, I'm extremely fortunate to have made a film under that regime, under that—it's hard to explain to anyone who has never worked in the old Disney studio. There was so much, it was such a lovely place. Beautifully maintained. And there were only four or five soundstages and one of them was given over to the blue screen stuff.

"They were very careful. They would call and say we need to reshoot this scene because the way you said that line was not quite right. Or that your look: You were talking on the telephone, and you were talking to the bishop and you rolled your eyes, and we don't want to give any impression that the guy was saying something I was very impatient with. From a character point of view, it made perfect sense what I was doing, but Disney required that you didn't show disrespect to anybody's church hierarchy. So, I was to tone down that reaction and it was a non-verbal reaction, but we had to reshoot that. We had to go back, regress, shoot that scene. And of course, again, I was steaming. You know, how dare they! It's my role, it's my acting! Then no, no, Walt's still here. Just do it the way they want it to be done. Just shut up, Hermann."

Rev. Hill makes acquaintances with Anne Woods (Susan Clark), the daughter of the former head of the church. Anne resents Hill's presence and warns him that the parishioners are unreliable when it comes to committees and volunteer work. To prove her wrong, Hill immediately tasks Mrs. Rafferty (Patsy Kelly) with leading the "sinking fund" (basically the church's 'rainy day' money).

"Start thinking of ways of building up the fund," he tells her. Mrs. Rafferty's methodology is less-than-sound, allowing her husband to bet the entire fund on a horse race. When Hill tries to rescind the bet, he runs into the first underworld character in the film, Harry the Hat (Alan Hale Jr), who manages to trick Hill out of his money and his pants.

Humiliated and broke, Rev. Hill tries to oust the extensive underworld presence in the city only to find that the police and city officials are in cahoots with the mob. Rev. Hill appeals to the community at large via a local television broadcast but the people of New Camden choose to ignore his pleas. Instead, he's raked over the coals by his own Presbyterian executive, Dr. Fulton (Herb Voland). Meanwhile, many members of his community consider him "a nut."

Under cover of darkness, Rev. Hill is approached by Agents Marv Fogleman (Michael Constantine) and Tom Voorhies (Steve Franken) of the U.S. Treasury Department who want to help him take down the mob. After striking out with the city's leading citizens, Rev. Hill realizes he has a group of five dedicated ladies (and one gentleman) who will help. "Who would suspect a bunch of dingaling dames?" Fogleman wonders.

This sequence of the ladies attempting to place bets and follow various "bag men" around the city becomes the meat of the movie which now belongs to the female leads.

"It was a collection of crazy ladies," recalls Herrmann. Barbara Harris (in a very unconvincing wig) plays Vickie, the harried mother driving around a group of wild children (some of her own). Karen Valentine is Jane, who always seems to be in the wrong with her future mother-in-law (mother nature herself, Dena Dietrich). Virginia Capers is Cleo, the only person of color in the film apart from her infant son. Her (never seen) husband sells used cars and supplies her with some unreliable models with which to track down the mob money men. Patsy Kelly (Mrs. Rafferty) and Douglas Fowley (Mr. Rafferty) are a salty Irish couple. And, finally, Cloris Leachman is Claire, a kooky spinster with talon-like nails and a penchant for wild outfits.

Bruce Bilson recalls, "Everybody got along. Cloris is wonderful but a handful. Not mean, but a handful. With that wardrobe, we'd go, 'Oh, that's good.' But she'd go and change again, then say, 'Wait a minute, you know I can change this. Did you like the other one? Maybe I could put...' It went on like that for six hours. Twice. Tom and I came out and I said, 'That is the worst day of prep I ever spent, in my career!' Exhausting. She could exhaust you.

"You know, she's got a mind that goes everywhere at once, and it was really fun watching her in this movie, because boy, she was always in there. The biggest joke in the movie, for me, was when she broke her fingernails. That was her idea, I think. That was one of those things that came to happen because she made the fingernails that way, that's who she wanted to be."

Edward Herrmann adds, "What can I say and be polite? It was an amazing display of feminine behavior. Let's put a vanilla word on it. Watching them deal with Cloris. Cloris is absolutely brilliant, she has given some of the great film performances of all time, but she was a very, very difficult character. She was a loose cannon. And she would keep everybody waiting, she'd do all kinds of crazy stuff. And show up—if the call was at 8, she'd show up at 11, and brought out a great big pot of something to make for everyone, because everyone looked tired. She was always ingratiating herself with the crew... just crazy.

"Virginia [Capers] was one that was most annoyed by Cloris. She'd get steamy. Storm off. I, I'd just keep to my knitting and kept my mouth shut."

Herrmann fondly recalls working with Douglas Fowley who had once been a dashing leading man, "I just loved Douglas. He was so full of stories and I lapped them up. I recognize the behavior now, because kids will come to me and they'll ask me questions and I'll tell a story and they either get bored with it or ask more. It makes you feel that you have something to pass on, you have something of interest to pass on and you might actually do the kid some help, talking about actors that you've known, experiences you've had. You're just spinning a tale, being entertaining. He was full of the most wonderful stories, because he worked in the golden period. He was in everything from *Battleground* where he's clicking his teeth, with Van Johnson, and over at MGM he played Boston Blackie. He was a very, very useful character man."

The North Avenue Irregulars marked the second time that Bruce Bilson would work with Fowley, "I met him when I was Assistant Director, actually Second Assistant Director, on *The Life and Legend of Wyatt Earp* in the '50s. He had been a handsome, leading man kind of bad guy, good guy, with a neat little mustache. He had a gag, he would take his teeth out and be this other old guy. He just played the hell out of being in drag."

The film's tour de force finale culminates in what can be best described as a "smash up derby" wherein the aforementioned "Irregulars" (now with Anne Woods as part of the team) break the mob's "bank" and take down the local kingpin, Max Rocha (Frank Campanella) in a fit of vehicular mayhem.

Recalls Bilson, "We had a big budget for cars. Cloris drove a Lincoln Continental. We had two of those—we had at least two of everything. Had that old Jaguar that we banged up. Barbara had her station wagon. And the black lady, her husband owned a used car lot, so we got to make up all the things to put on the windows."

The smash-up scene includes a great appearance by Ruth Buzzi as Dr. Rheems, a Lady Breaker (female CB enthusiast).

All is well that ends well with *The North Avenue Irregulars* though things wrap up a little too quickly. The single Rev. Hill is paired with Anne Woods, the church is saved, and the mob is defeated.

Ultimately, critics damned the film with faint praise. Oddly, multiple writers criticized the demolition derby as "bloodless!" The film's more adult theme of taking on the mob surprised some audiences but at least one critic described the film's audience as "howl[ing] with glee throughout the show with the adults joining their children in waves of laughter."

Today the film is almost forgotten except by those people who saw the movie in early 1979.

AIRPLANE II: THE SEQUEL

by Mike White

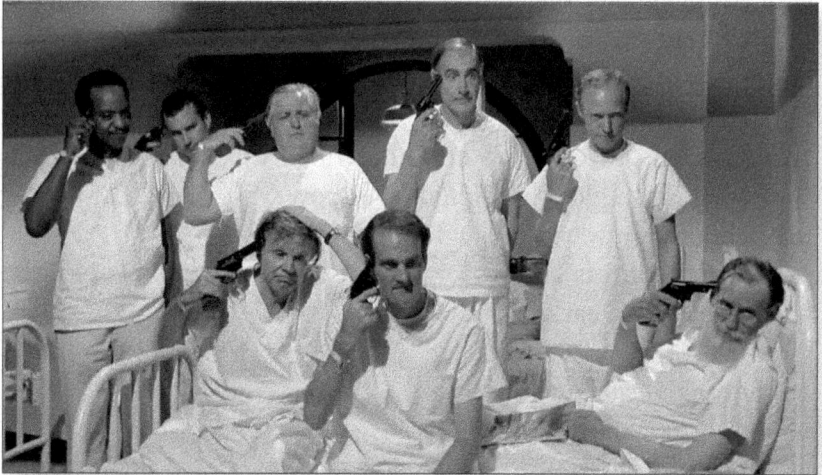

(All Airplane II *photos from the author's collection)*

With an estimated budget of $3.5 million and grosses over $158 million,[1] a sequel to 1980's *Airplane* was inevitable. Unfortunately for Paramount Pictures, *Airplane*'s writer/director team of Jim Abrahams, David Zucker and Jerry Zucker had no interest in creating another (they would later have no such qualms when making sequels for *Hot Shots* or *The Naked Gun*).

"They had already done *Airplane*," explained executive producer Howard W. Koch, "and they felt they couldn't top it. They didn't want to be criticized for trying and they weren't interested in the money."[2]

Ken Finkleman was in the right place at the right time. A native of Winnipeg, Manitoba, Finkleman wrote, produced and performed a half-hour political news satire program for Canadian

---

1 Nancy Mills, "Airplane II - Zany again, but will it fly?" *San Francisco Chronicle,* 5 December 1982
2 Ibid

Broadcasting Corporation (CBC) radio with Rick Moranis which lead to a Finkleman-Moranis television pilot.

Finkleman went to New York in the early '80s where he toiled on another news satire show for ABC that didn't go anywhere. "I believe it was a Lorne Michaels production. One of the writers in the room was Abbie Hoffman," says Finkelman. "One of them was Jeff Greenfield who's now a political analyst on NBC. Another guy was Christopher Cerf who's the son of Bennett Cerf, the head of Random House. I'm pretty sure Tony Hendra, the guy who played the manager in *This is Spinal Tap*, was in the room as well." (This would follow as Hendra had worked with Cerf on *Not the New York Times*).

"It was pulled by Fred Silverman. This was right around the time of the assassination attempt on Ronald Reagan [March 30, 1981]. Silverman pulled it because he thought the show was another kind of attack on Reagan."

After this gig, Finkleman did a rewrite for another oft-maligned sequel, *Grease 2*. The original writers took their names off the project leaving Finkleman sole credit (and the residual checks). The final draft of the *Grease 2* script is dated October 28, 1981.

"I wasn't doing very much," Finkleman says, "I was unemployed and living in New York. I was in an office in New York talking to a woman about some project or something. She gets a phone call while I'm sitting there talking to her. It's from these two guys from Toronto, Steve Kampmann and Peter Torokvei. I'd used Kampmann in a TV pilot I did for the CBC. He was a character in it. They were out in L.A. working on a sequel to *Airplane*.

"So, the phone rings in this woman's office and she says, 'I have someone else from Toronto here.' She put me on the phone and we started chatting and comparing notes. They asked me if I would work with them. After they got the approval of the Paramount, they shipped me out there to L.A. where I started working with them by the pool at Peter's house.

"Paramount had signed up three different pairs of writers to write scripts to see which one was best. To put teams of writers in a race is somewhat frowned upon by the Writers Guild of America, unless you notify the writing parties. So, everyone knew that they were in a bit of a horserace here. Steve and Peter were one of the teams going for it and they had gotten nowhere.

"They wanted to do something completely different. I told them, 'You guys, I don't know anything about the movie business but I think that when they're doing a sequel, they want to come very close to what was done before! They don't want something different. This isn't just my cynicism coming into play here. They want the same thing! Let's copy the jokes.'

The original *Airplane* parodied Hall Bartlett's *Zero Hour* which was also the basis for George Seaton's *Airport*. Released in 1970, *Airport* was the highest-grossing film of the year and one of several star-studded disaster films of the era (*The Towering Inferno*, *The Poseidon Adventure*). It spawned several sequels which raised the stakes by putting an airplane into increasingly perilous situations. The series ended with David Lowell Rich's *The Concorde...Airplane '79* (not to be confused with Italian knock-off *Concorde Affaire '79*).

Likewise, the sequel to *Airplane* had to be bigger and more outrageous. Going faster than a Concorde and cashing in on first launch of the Space Shuttle Colombia (April 12, 1981), *Airplane 2* would center on an ill-fated shuttle flight. "That was from the studio," says Finkleman. "It was a dumb fucking idea, to tell you the truth. But, what am I going to do? They're paying me money and I got a door open to being in Hollywood.

"We worked for a couple of weeks and we got nowhere. I told Steve and Peter to keep working on the script in L.A. but I was going home to work on my own.

"I got back to Toronto and started pecking away at this thing on an old Selectric. I got a phone call from Kampmann a few weeks later where he told me that his partner wanted to bail and proposed that I write the stuff and that he'll edit me. I told him that I wasn't familiar with the industry in Los Angeles but that I also wasn't born yesterday. I immediately got on the phone with the executive on the project, Jeff Katzenberg. I told him that I came in late to the project and I didn't quite know what to do, except that I wasn't going to get fucked over by anyone. I told him that I would continue the work if I could continue on my own. Katzenberg told me to hang up and he called me back in about ten minutes to tell me that those guys were gone and to send him what I had so far.

"I told him that what I had was only cut and pasted. Remember, this was the time of true cutting and pasting where you cut the paper and you'd take Scotch tape and paste them in order onto a clean sheet of paper. I told him, 'I don't know what I have here. I don't even know if it's a movie. I've got fifty pages of jokes.' He said, 'Just send it to us FedEx.' A couple days after I sent it I got a phone call from them telling me to come back to L.A. to finish it. When I went through the gate at Paramount, I said to myself, 'You're over the wall and it will take all the King's horses to get you out,' and that's when I knew I was in. That's how I came to Hollywood."

THE HOLLYWOOD GAME

Work on the script began in earnest in the early months of 1982.

The plot of *Airplane II: The Sequel* retreads much of *Airplane* with an estranged Elaine Dickinson (Julie Hagerty) about to fly away from Ted Striker (Robert Hayes) on a ship piloted by Captain Clarence Oveur (Peter Graves).

In the years between the two films, Elaine left the unstable Ted and got engaged to Simon Kurtz (Chad Everett), a cocky pilot in the pocket of the businessmen pushing for the shuttle's launch despite it being a buggy deathtrap. In a flashback, we see Simon disparaging Ted's reputation at a trial about the crash of the XR-2300 test shuttle.

Ted gets thrown back into the loony bin. When he learns that the *Mayflower I* has been green lit for launch he promptly escapes, determined to stop the shuttle's flight to the moon and to win back Elaine.

During the flight, the *Mayflower*'s computerized navigation system, ROC 4000 (voiced by Finkleman), goes berserk, leaving the flight without a pilot. It's up to Ted Striker to save the day... once again. Little does anyone know that there's another wrinkle to the *Mayflower*'s maiden flight, passenger Joe Seluchi (Sonny Bono) has brought a bomb aboard.

Meanwhile, back on Earth, Steve McCroskey (Lloyd Bridges) returns to take charge of the tower while Commander Buck Murdock

(William Shatner) takes over the Rex Kramer (Robert Stack) role from the original *Airplane*, barking out orders at Striker as he tries to safely land the *Mayflower* on the moon.

The Zucker/Abrahams/Zucker team had five years to write, rewrite, polish and tighten the script for *Airplane*. Finkleman had five months. More than that, he also had Paramount executives breathing down his neck. "I had no control of the script. I got two writers to come in from the east, Mike Reiss and Al Jean from the *Harvard Lampoon*. They helped me with the script but I never ended up using any of their stuff, but we still became good friends. It was their first job in Hollywood and they ended up becoming producers on *The Simpsons*."

Robert Hays remembers, "When we were doing the second Airplane, Ken would ask me to come in while he was writing it because I had already had the experience with the first one. I would go over to the studio where he was working and I'd just laugh my butt off, he was a very funny guy."

Says Finkleman, "The thing is, I have this quirk and it's something that draws a lot of guys to Hollywood. I can write jokes. It's just a quirky thing. Someone could tell me to, I don't know, write ten jokes about a glass of water, and I could do it."

"Ken was fun," Hays recalls, "He was a bit hyper at times. I think he was under a lot of pressure. I remember he came into the office one day before we started the film and he looked very flustered, like

he'd been through the ringer. He put his briefcase down and I asked him, 'What's the matter?'

"He said, 'Finally, I think I figured out the definition of making a film in Hollywood: making the deal is like having sex with the girl. Making the movie is like trying to get her out of your apartment.'"

The second draft of the script (dated February 18, 1982) resembles the final film in many ways with approximately half of the scenes and jokes remaining intact. The other half contains several hilarious sequences including Striker flying into the South American town of Palukaville to escape his troubles. He lays in his hot, dusty room at the Hotel Montenegro, ruminating on his problems with a crucifix above his bed; a full-size crucifix with a man nailed to it. A few of the jokes in this sequence would find a home in the final draft when Striker is in the Ronald Reagan Institute for the Mentally Feeble.

There's also a Ronald Reagan Institute of Supply-Side Economics where we see the white version of Sammy Davis Jr. and economist David Stockman incessantly muttering, "It does work... No, it doesn't."

Finkleman included several recurring characters throughout this draft that didn't survive subsequent rounds including a Steinbeckian Okie family who count on Mercury to be a land of opportunity, a dour Swedish family called "The Bergmans" who feel Mercury is "a whole new world to be depressed about," a world-famous agronomist and his daughter, and a trio of terrorists. There are also running gags about Elaine constantly feeding spaghetti to Striker and a crisis about the coffee machine (including an appearance by Joe Dimaggio, Mr. Coffee himself).

Ironically, the Joe Seluchi character is described as being like Van Heflin and his wife like Cher. This is before Cher's ex-husband, Sonny Bono, was cast.

In a genre where cutting remarks can be hidden by the veil of comedy, several jokes were sacrificed after being deemed unacceptable. "There was a joke where they were about to crash and the flight attendants were taking a poll of the passengers and her last question was, 'Should America get out of Nicaragua?' and [Michael] Eisner killed that joke," says Finkleman. "I had all these political jokes that came out of nowhere. Katzenberg was violently right wing.

"You have to understand, I come from a left wing political background. I went to university with all of these guys from Winnipeg which was kind of a hotbed of North American socialism. We're all opposed to The System and I'm right in the fucking belly of it.

"You don't ask questions in Hollywood. You don't argue in Hollywood. In writers' meetings you just nod your head. They're paying you a shitload of money to do something you don't have any connection to at all. You don't feel any pride in anything. I always said that if I'm going to be there that I'm never going to be in the position where I have to defend anything I've written because I will lose the fight. I decided to write stupid, silly stuff, take the money, and run."

The script went through several revisions. The front cover of the May 28, 1982 reads "Absolutely the Very Last Draft." Filming began after the Memorial Day weekend on Wednesday June 2 with an eight week shooting schedule and an $8 million budget[1] with Ken Finkleman at the helm.

---

1 Ibid

FINDING THE DIRECTOR

"I'm a very ambitious character by nature," says Finkleman. "I finished the script; after rewrite after rewrite after rewrite. Then one day, Michael Eisner comes into an office where I'm sitting with another executive, Larry Marks. The offices at Paramount are kind of small. They were in an old building from the old days. The executives went from junior executives, then Katzenberg (who was still kind of a junior executive) and then Don Simpson who was president of production, and then Eisner was above him in another office and Berry Diller was at the end of the hall. So, Eisner comes in with a script in his hand and he asks, 'Who can we get to do this script?' Marks points at me and says, 'Give it to him.' Eisner hands me the script and says, 'Read it tonight.'

"It was a script they wanted to do with John Belushi. It was *The Joy of Sex* and it was shitty. Horrible. Stupid. The next day I was supposed to come to Eisner's office and I was an hour and a half late. He was pissed off but what did I know? I was from the '60s and '70s. I didn't have any respect for authority. I was out of Winnipeg and didn't give a fuck about these guys, right? I'm not being flip about this, I really had that attitude. It was really a defining thing in my mind to not suck up to these guys. The funny thing is that at the end of the day you end up in the same position whether you suck up to these guys or not.

"I moseyed into his office and Eisner asked me, 'Will you do this?' and I told him that I was rewriting *Airplane II*. 'No, no,' he said, 'Will you direct it? Larry told me that you could direct.'

"I said, 'Direct?! I don't know one end of the camera from the other.'

"He said, 'You're not going to do this?'

"I told him that I wasn't going to direct *The Joy of Sex* and I left. But, still, in his mind I'm a director who has passed on him, not a writer who was mistaken for a director. Thus, when the script for *Airplane II* is finished he said, 'See if you can get Finkleman to direct it.' So, I did it.

"Now, they tested me. They gave me a couple of scenes and I basically had to point the camera at the people who were talking. I passed the test, apparently, because they said 'Okay, do it.'

"I did it and I hated every second of it.

"I was shooting a picture on the Paramount lot and every day I wanted to walk off it. Every time I went to take a leak, I just wanted to keep on walking. I don't think I was ever more insane in my whole life, feeling the pressure. Every morning Katzenberg would call me into his office at 7:30 to beat me up about the dailies. It wouldn't have bothered me if it was something important but it was so trite! That's what drove me insane, that it was so meaningless. It was less than meaningless."

As to directing actors, Finkleman recalls, "I had the sense that I knew what I was doing. You kind of just let people do what they do. I really haven't changed that much, even today, in how I deal with actors. If they're doing something completely wrong, you try to help them along."

"I remember Julie Hagerty being very nervous. I was a complete novice and had never been involved in the business, of course. I joked around with her by faking being mad with her on the set. I grabbed her and mimed slapping her in the face. She kind of thought that was funny and it broke the ice because it was something that I really didn't have the right to do since she had been in the first one. She really seemed to be a nice person."

Most of the central cast of *Airplane* returned for *Airplane II* with the notable exception of Leslie Nielsen. By March of 1982, Nielsen was appearing in the next Zucker/Abrahams/Zucker project, *Police Squad*. This tragically short-lived television series had only six episodes spread out between March 4 and July 8. Much of the material of *Police Squad* would be recycled for the *Naked Gun* films.

THAT'S A WRAP

Released December 10, 1982 – approximately 18 months after *Airplane's* opening date -- the poster for *Airplane II* featured a flaming plane, its wings tied in knots, pulling a frantic Santa Claus on his sleigh through the air. The tagline reads, "For the ride of your life... All you need for Christmas are your two front seats!"

A survey of reviews paints a dismal critical response to the film. However, the jury may have been rigged. "Three weeks [before the release of *Airplane II*], the nation's film critics received letters from a Los Angeles public relations agency, advising [the press] that their clients David Zucker, Jim Abrahams and Jerry Zucker, the makers of the original *Airplane*, had no connection with the sequel."[1]

1 Vincent Canby, "Airplane II: Sequel Focuses on Lunar Shuttle" *New York Times*, 10 December 1982

Roger Ebert liked the bare boobs. "The gags involving the metal-detectors, the check-in counter and the passenger-unloading zone are really funny." He enjoyed the film's first ten minutes but bemoaned "*Airplane II* never really seems to know whether it's about a spaceship. It's all sight gags, one-liners, puns, funny signs and scatological cross-references. There's no story. I'm not saying a movie this silly needs to have a story, but it wouldn't have hurt."[1]

Vincent Canby wrote that *Airplane II* was so "shamelessly, tirelessly inferior to the original that it's almost appealing. It's a Saville Row suit made in Hong Kong."[2]

In *The Hollywood Reporter*, Tina Daniell wrote "*Airplane II* hits fewer high points than its predecessor, perhaps since it replays some of the same jokes in terms of both character conceits and routines, and unspools at an overall slower pace."[3]

The reviewer at *Film Journal International* called the film "a loser" with "a string of unfunny gags and adolescent jokes [that] exploits the original without adding ingenuity or imagination of its own."[4]

Variety damned the film saying, "At best, Finkleman has managed to match the spirit of the first venture but implants no recognizable imprint of his own for wit and imagination. And, none of his new cameoed characters, unfortunately, is equal as replacement for those now missing. What's worse about '*II*' is that it is so structurally the same as '*I*' that everything it attempts reminds how much better it seemed the first time. It makes no real difference that it's now a space shuttle in trouble instead of an airplane; essentially the same people are on board and the same types down below trying to get the aircraft home safely."[5]

IN SPACE NO ONE CAN HEAR YOU LAUGH

Despite its setting, *Airplane II* does not play like a science fiction film. Indeed, its suspect layout of the solar system put many view-

---

1 Roger Ebert, "Airplane II - The Sequel" *Chicago Sun Times*, 13 December 1982
2 Vincent Canby, "Airplane II: Sequel Focuses on Lunar Shuttle" *New York Times*, 10 December 1982
3 Tina Daniell, "Airplane II - The Sequel" *Hollywood Reporter*, 8 December 1982
4 S.C., "Airplane II - The Sequel" *Film Journal International*, 27 December, 1982
5 Har., "Airplane II - The Sequel" *Variety*, 8 December 1982

ers in a tizzy. When it's shown that the *Mayflower I* is traveling through an asteroid belt it would seem that the ship has shot past the moon and bypassed Mars, moving through the asteroid belt that separates the inner planets and the gas giants. To then learn that the *Mayflower I* will collide with the sun means that it's going in the opposite direction.

The "it's-the-same-but-it's-different"[1] ploy distressed some viewers who thought of *Airplane II* as more of a remake than a sequel. As *Airplane* parodied the *Airport* films as well as several other '70s favorites (*Saturday Night Fever*, etc.), the outer space setting of *Airplane II* should have provided a vast array of science fiction films from the previous decade to mock (*Alien, Star Wars, The Alpha Incident*, et cetera). Even as *Airplane* concentrated on directly parodying *Zero Hour* (down to identical compositions and camera angles), *Airplane II* could have taken more of its source inspiration from another film, apart from *Airplane*.

---

1 Nancy Mills, "Airplane II - Zany again, but will it fly?" *San Francisco Chronicle*, 5 December 1982

Certainly there were some missed opportunities such as a more overt parody of *2001: A Space Odyssey*. After dispatching the flight crew and locking the navigation controls ROC drops out of the story. A disengaging of ROC similar to Dave Bowman "killing" HAL 9000 and learning of the true nature of the Jupiter mission could have provided some laughs as well as a resolution to the Bud Kruger storyline.

Even with these detractions, *Airplane II* has its fans and for good reason. Had Finkleman not had to deal with meddling from Paramount executives worries about their potential cash cow, the fledgling director might have pulled off quite a coup; creating a sequel of equal weight to the original film. Finkleman knew to keep the jokes coming fast and furious. The second draft of the script evidences the right mix of surrealism, slapstick, and solid humor.

One of the most divisive roles of *Airplane II* also managed to become its longest-lasting legacy. Appearing as Commander Buck Murdoch (perhaps a distant relative to Roger Murdoch in the original *Airplane*), William Shatner was both praised ("The funniest performance is turned in by William Shatner"[1]) and lambasted ("Among those with too much to do is William Shatner")[2] by critics for his performance.

This was one of several turning points in William Shatner's career. March of 1982 brought *T.J. Hooker* to the small screen and *Star Trek II: The Wrath of Khan* to the big screen three months later. But, despite some ludicrous roles, *Airplane II* was the first time Shatner overtly satirized himself.

Says Finkleson, "He's made a career out of kind of that. He even wrote an autobiography and he never mentioned that I was the one to get him to do it. That was the very first time he ever satirized his over-the-top Shakespearian/Captain Kirk pausing style and I got him to do it for *Airplane II*. He hadn't done it before and he made an industry out of afterward. He never gave me credit because I don't think he liked me. I don't think we got along very well while we were doing the film."

---

1 Tina Daniell, "Airplane II - The Sequel" *Hollywood Reporter*, 8 December 1982

2 Har., "Airplane II - The Sequel" *Variety*, 8 December 1982

Shatner gets the last line of *Airplane II* when the end credits announce that *Airplane III* would be coming soon, "That's exactly what they'll be expecting us to do."

When asked if there would be an *Airplane III* shortly before the release of *Airplane II* Ken Finkleman stated, "In terms of money, [...] it makes sense to do as many sequels as possible – until they stop being successful."[1] Despite being lambasted by the critics, with a budget of $8 million and grosses over $27 million, *Airplane II* was ultimately a success. Yet, *Airplane III* has yet to materialize.

It would be three years before Finkleman directed another film, *Head Office*. Eventually he packed his bags and headed back to native Canada. "Many years after *Airplane II*, my wife and I went to law school and she became a judge. Looking at my job in Hollywood—and this is why I got out—I used to say, 'My wife's trying to decide whether to put a young guy in jail or not and in Hollywood I'm trying to decide whether to dress the guy in the bear costume or the gorilla costume.'"

INTERVIEW WITH ROBERT HAYS

Were you ever afraid that you were going to get typecast as a "Ted Striker Type"?

Oh, yeah, I did. I mean the press, when I would go to an opening of a film or some event or something would all be like, "Hey, Robert 'Airplane' Hays, you think you'll ever do anything besides *Airplane*? Are you going to be a *real* actor?" They were ruthless. Back then it was frowned-upon to do sequels. Nowadays they call it a franchise. That's why I turned down *Airplane III* because I was just hounded by that. I wish I had done the third one. It would have been fun to have the three of them.

It's ironic that you did Airplane II *and didn't get typecast. Meanwhile, Leslie Nielson didn't do the film but ended up doing all those zany parody movies.*

That's what he really loved. Leslie used to say that [Zucker/Abrahams/Zucker] opened the door for him to step into this kind

---

1 Nancy Mills, "Airplane II - Zany again, but will it fly?" *San Francisco Chronicle*, 5 December 1982

of insanity and then they gave him a gentle nudge through the door. And once they did that, he just took off.

Was there any animosity between you and the Zucker/Abrahams/ Zucker team because you did the sequel?

I know they didn't want to do the movie, but they told me that I could finally make some money if I did the sequel because I got chicken feed from the first one.

How did you manage to get through takes without laughing?

I came from theater. I was fairly fresh out of it. I mean, maybe ten years or less out of it but, still, fairly trained and I could keep a straight face. What we used to do on stage if you had a show that was running – and, yes, I know this is very unprofessional – but when you're doing three shows a day, sometimes nine shows a week, you have one day off and you're just going nuts! After a while you've got people who start pulling pranks. The audience doesn't know what's going on but you know. They're trying to crack you up.

Keeping a straight face on *Airplane* wasn't much of a problem but it sure was enjoyable because everyone else was laughing. If I could get the crew to crack up then I knew it was good. I felt like I'd really accomplished something if they'd mess the take up. But, still, that was okay. We'd do it again and that was fine.

It's strange to think that the whole time you were doing the Airplane *films that you never really got to interact with some of the lead actors; Lloyd Bridges, Robert Stack, William Shatner, et cetera.*

Yeah, they were all on other sets. We were just supposedly talking but it was the script supervisor that would be talking to you, reading the lines. When they were shooting that stuff I used to go over to the other set and I'd read the lines off camera. I always liked to have the actors there so I figured they would, too.

By no means was I on a lonely set. We had all of the passengers that we were working with.

And you got to work with Sonny Bono!

Sonny! Well, I knew Sonny. We were at a lot of celebrity events and I used to go hang out with him at his restaurant. Good guy.

It was interesting to see him play a deranged terrorist.

Oh, yeah. I'd like a candy bar, a magazine, and the third bomb on the left. Did you notice the poster behind him?

Of Rocky XXXVIII*?*

Yeah! It's really hard to tell but the credits on the poster have everything inverted. You figure the lowliest guy on the crew is the craft service person and we had an old-time guy who wasn't fancy. He just made coffee and threw out doughnuts. His name was Art 'Klondike' Jones. He was just, "Take it or leave it." He was so funny but he was like an institution so Howard (W. Koch) hired him on the show. Well, if you look closely at the credits on *Rocky XXXVIII* you'll see that the executive producer is Klondike Jones and then it goes down from there; the lesser jobs are all at the top as producers, writers, directors, all of them. And then the lowliest, the craft services, is Howard W. Koch.

What are your feelings today about Airplane II*?*

I wish they'd re-release with outtakes, you know, deleted scenes. They did that with the first one but not with the second one. I wish they'd make a box set, actually, but I think having been two different writer/director teams that would probably make that difficult. We even had a gag reel that they put together. I love gag reels and I think that they should put that on the DVD, too. Even if that's too hard I wish they'd release the second one with deleted scenes. I think they'd sell a lot.

THE DELETED SCENES

Network broadcasts of *Airplane II* suffered from several cuts. Obviously, these omitted the bare breasted women on the TSA monitors and the jiggly juggy demonstrating the ship shimmying and shaking in a "Moral Majority" t-shirt (an uncredited Kitten Natividad). Also eliminated are the French kiss between a nun and Father O'Flanagan (James Noble), the anal retentive mental patient, a question to an information desk agent about faking orgasms, a discussion of "blowing" ROC, the deaf interpreter making an obscene gesture, implied donkey sex, Elaine smoking pot, and a joke about "premature ejection."

Additionally, a few cuts prove more perplexing than dirty such as the eggs frying on the control panel, Elaine's exchange with the passengers about the state of the ship, and some of Jacobs's funnier lines ("How about a show just like *Hollywood Squares* but with kids. Gary Coleman could host.")

These same broadcasts also boast several deleted scenes. In order, they are as follows:

• "Cut Rate Air" passengers being off-loaded from their flight by an attendant (John Paragon) pushing out the parachuting patrons.

• A Texan (Hugh Gillin) giving a thousand dollars to a man soliciting for a heart charity who subsequently has a heart attack.

• More of Striker's escape from the Ronald Regan Home for the Mentally Feeble; an orderly finds the newspaper that Dr. Stone (John Vernon) had given Striker with the headline "Elaine on Shuttle Too!" circled in black marker. A life-size Striker replica lay under the covers of his bed.

• An introduction to Joe Seluchi buying a ticket at the "No Class" line. In the second draft of the script this is described as "Travelers in line all wear gaudy double-knit suits, white belts and shoes, carry lava lamps and bongo drums, wear alpine hats, etc. The agent hands a no class traveler his ticket with large foam dice dangling." Joe carries these foam dice as he talks to his wife (Lee Purcell). Here we learn that Joe is headed to a clinic for impotence. As she talks about "their" needs as a couple, she paws unconsciously at a man in line (Craig Berenson). Before he leaves, he gives his wife an envelope. Later, we find that this is insurance.

• A controller (John Hancock) reports "Condition Green" while his green-faced coworker (Frank Ashmore) gets a few pills from a doctor. In the second draft of the script, this was the sole appearance of Dr. Rumack (Leslie Neilson). This role went to Earl Boen. "Here's some water," he says. "What is it, doctor?" asks the controller. "Two parts oxygen, one part hydrogen. It'll make the pills go down easier."

• Flight Attendant Mary (Wendy Phillips) offering some light reading to the Texan and Striker. The Texan opts for the Talmud while Striker opens up a copy of *Modern Electronics* that shorts out in his face. In the second draft of the screenplay the Talmud joke goes on further with several scenes of the Texan turning into a Hassidic Rabbi. In his final appearance he's completely entangled in tefillin.

• Captain Oveur ordering some breakfast from Flight Attendant Testa (Laurene Landon) via the ship's intercom with several mistaken interpretations of "Over" and "Oveur." "I don't think we do poached eggs on toast over, Captain Oveur. Over."

• Another appearance from Testa as she serves hot coffee to Mr. & Mrs. Waters (Howard Honig and Mary Mercier) before dropping the pot on Mrs. Waters's lap when she sees Navigator Dave Unger (Kent McCord) trying to come back on the ship. This bit must have been in the version shown to the press as Nancy Mills writes about it, "The stewardess grabs hold of his sleeve. She tugs and tugs and miraculously pulls him back into the ship – except that she's only rescued his jacket. The poor pilot! The stewardess desperately tugs some more and reels in a clothesline full of shirts and underwear."[1]

• The introduction of Steve McCroskey (Lloyd Bridges) shows two nurses getting a call from the space center. "Do you think we should bother him? He's been acting a bit odd lately," the main nurse (Louise Sorel) says. They find McCroskey under the covers of his bed, only a snorkel sticking out. "He's fine. He just thinks he's Lloyd Bridges." The nurse puts a hand over the snorkel to get him out from "underwater." After talking to the controllers he gets out of bed saying, "Looks like I picked the wrong time to go senile."

• A female controller tries to reach *Mayflower 1* without any luck. McCroskey tries it, throwing down the microphone in disgust. Another controller makes an attempt, crashing the mic through a monitor when he fails. Another controller takes an axe to the computer banks asking, "Come in *Mayflower 1*." The camera tracks

---

1   Nancy Mills, "Airplane II - Zany again, but will it fly?" *San Francisco Chronicle*, 5 December 1982

along a line of armed controllers waiting their turn to take a swing at the smoking and flaming computers.

• As the ship hurtles toward the sun the temperature inside increases. According to the ship's navigational controls, the estimated distance to the sun is 161749578.01 and the exact distance is 76.05. The passengers are dropping like flies from the heat, replete with buzzing sound effects. There are even two old men (Martin Garner and Jack Bernardi) having a nice schvitz while talking real estate.

• Finally coming back into the film, Sarge (Chuck Connors) goes over the *Mayflower 1* plans, explaining what might happen if a bomb were to go off inside. "If you blast here in the computer core and the fuselage doesn't give way here and the main communication lines to the cockpit hold here and this baby here doesn't jam this little old unit up here and throw about two tons of hot steel through here like a hot knife through butter and the upper and lower..." McCrosky interrupts him asking, "What's your point, Sarge?" "I have no point."

In the second draft of the script the scene continues with McCrosky saying, "Then it's settled. The bomb is Striker's only chance. Are there any questions?" When the controllers have none he chides, "Those are answers, I asked for questions." Finally, one asks, "Should a man in his forties have a circumcision?" "Absolutely."

• After Joe Seluchi is disarmed, Striker brings the bomb to the cockpit. Elaine lets ground control know that they have the bomb. The news gets passed from one controller to another, "They've got the bomb!" until it reached Jacobs who exclaims, "This is just like an election in Iran!"

• The Commissioner (John Dehner) phones the president to inform him of the situation. Cut to the President (Rip Torn in a double role as a thinly veiled Reagan) who poses for a photo session. He holds aloft in a victory salute, the hands of two black men as an off-screen photographer says, "One for the NAACP, Mr. President." On the camera flash we loosen to reveal the bodiless arms of two black mannequins. An aide hands the phone to the President who says, "Frank, we'd better go to split screen." The screen splits to show Reagan on the left and The Commissioner on the right. Barely visible in the background is an Arab piling cash onto the President's desk.

The Commissioner says, "I don't think that shuttle's going to make it, sir." The President replies, "Damn it, Mister, the dignity and integrity of this presidency depends on the success of that mission. Now, I don't want to hear from you again until that thing's safely on the moon."

In the second draft screenplay (where the story is set in 2002), the President "walks past a series of photographs on his way to the phone: JFK, Johnson, Nixon, Ford, Carter, Reagan, Reagan older, Reagan much older, Merv Griffin, a chimp, and this President."

The screenplay also outlines the President's further strategy in dealing with the situation: "I work for the people of these United States, Frank. I have to do what's best for them." He grabs the red phone and orders, "Al, kill social security, cancel school lunches only for the poor, dismantle welfare, close all hospitals and public toilets, green light the MX-6, invade Brazil, and bring my horse around after my nap!"

• Wearing a space suit, Simon prepares to use one of the shuttle's escape capsules. "I've lost my ship and now I've lost you, Elaine. I'm getting off." She tries to console him by telling him that they can still be friends, "We can meet for lunch or after work for a drink. I mean, I know now that Ted and I were always meant for each other. And, you'll meet somebody. And then we can all double date!" He gets into the capsule telling her that he can't hack the singles scene again.

The above were shown on television but a few more scenes remain extant but unavailable.

• In the *Airplane II* trailer is a bit of the scene where a couple argues with a desk clerk saying that they've lost their travelers' checks. A Karl Malden lookalike (Tom McGeevey) asks them what kind they were. "American Excess," they answer. "Then I'm afraid you're screwed," he replies, putting up his arms in the same pose as the "American Excess" poster behind him.

• Another scene in the trailer has Elaine telling Seluchi that he should put his case in the overhead compartment. When he defers she tells him, "Well, I can help you if you can't get it up."

• The trailer ends with a list of actors appearing in the film with two notably absent from the final cut of the film. Aldo Ray gets a mention here as well as in Nancy Mills's *San Francisco Chronicle* article, "Aldo Ray plays a sergeant major who during an emergency leads the passengers in songs such as 'Pack Your Troubles in Your Old Kit Bag.'" Says Finkleman, "I think he was singing 'New York, New York' as well. Back then I used to think of him as having a certain place in the iconography of American films. He was like the soldier in those Second World War movies. I think he was so bad in the movie that we cut him out." Yet, Ray's name remained in the movie listings for *Airplane II* in *New York Magazine* (December 13, 1982 – February 14, 1983).

• Sonny Bono's wife at the time, Susie Bono (née Coelho), also gets a mention in the credits (as well as a *New York Times* piece).[1] However, her role in the film is unknown and Ms. Bono was unreachable for comment.

• It's rumored that an airing of the film shortly after the official announcement of Ronald Reagan's Alzheimer's diagnosis changes the sign outside the Ronald Reagan Home for the Mentally Ill was changed to the "Donald Dragon" Home for the Mentally Ill.

The most involved lost sequence description comes courtesy of Robert Hays:

"There was an entire scene that was shot of when I was having my flashbacks. There was one where I was, you know, as usual, boring people to death. I was telling them about after all the stuff had happened in the first movie that Elaine and I had gotten married but I was just too antsy. I couldn't handle it and I left to join the French Foreign Legion. Because of my prior experience being in command and being an officer, I was put in command of a bunch of guys.

---

1 Janet Maslin, "Hollywood Has Something for Everyone" *New York Times*, 12 September 1982

"Then it started doing that time rippling effect where it goes back to us going across the sand dunes. We filmed it at the foot of LAX in all the sand dunes down there. It was me leading everybody with our French Foreign Legion outfits on—everyone behind me—this long line of guys trampling along. I hold my hand up and we all stop. I hold up my binoculars and I see a fort, a little small fort in the distance with palm trees. And I say, 'Come on, let's go!' and signal with my arm.

"We all keep marching and as we get closer and closer, we get right up next to it and it's a little, small fort. I mean, it's only about eight inches tall. I kind of stare at it before I pick up my binoculars and look at it and, sure enough, that's the one I saw.

"We just keep marching and we have a run-in with the Bedouins or whoever it is. And, because of my prior experience coming in too low; you know, 'You're coming in too low, Striker!' This time I swore I wouldn't come in too low. I yell, 'Charge!' and they insert this stock footage of all the Bedouin tribes fighting on horseback. And we all descend down the side of the sand dune and come in too high!

"I'm the only one left as I come crawling up over the top of the sand dune. I lost everybody. Donkeys, too. It's just me, now, and I'm walking along and you see my face, burning, parched and all the crinkles on my lips and everything. It cuts to the sun burning with that sizzling sun sound. We see my boots as I trample through the sand. Then you see my rifle butt dragging in the sand. They were filming this from about mid-thigh down. You see the rifle fall. And then you see the ammo belt fall. Now, I'm defenseless and it's really getting bad. Then you see the canteen fall. Then you know that I'm just really shot.

"And then an egg beater falls. Then a bowl. Then a rolling pin. Somebody was taking stills on the set and there's a shot of me with an armload of stuff that I was dropping bit by bit.

"Finally, I collapse in the sand and I get up to a watering hole that's all dried out. On the far side is a Texas longhorn steer skull which I'm wondering, 'What the hell's that doing in the Sudan?' I look up and there's a water cooler from an office and there are two skeletons dressed in three-piece suits with cups. They're standing there like they're having a little conversation. The water cooler is full of sand and the cups are full of sand.

"I roll over on my back like, 'Oh, God, this is over. This is it.' The sun is beating down and there's all this music to signal that I'm about to die from dehydration. And then I hear something.

"It was one of my favorite shots. The camera was down below my feet and it was shot up through my feet. My head pops up like, 'What the hell is that?' I just love that shot. I find enough strength to crawl over to the edge of the sand dune and there's the Pacific Ocean and there's the beach and there's a band – they're kind of a combination of The Beatles and The Beach Boys. They're playing music with electrified instruments. Where the hell is all that coming from? And there's everybody dancing and having a good time at a beach party!

"Elaine is there wearing this big one-piece bathing suit and we had Annette Funicello, the real Annette Funicello, in one of those old big wide bikinis where the bottoms are about a foot wide and the tops are about ten inches wide.

"I go running up to Elaine and say, 'Elaine, I've missed you. I was so wrong for leaving you!' And then I suddenly realize and ask, 'What the hell are you doing in the middle of the Sudan?'

"She says, 'Oh, Ted, you're so square!' and she makes a big rectangle with her fingers.

"Now, you can see in the background, just like the *Beach Blanket Bingo* movies, that there are maybe six-inch waves on the ocean. Somebody yells, 'Surf's up!' and all these people go running by her with surfboards. She puts her hands up on either side of her face like she's so excited and goes running off, leaving me standing there in my stringy, ragged, French Foreign Legion outfit. Annette Funicello comes up to me and starts singing one of those real sappy songs, 'If you want her, go and get her.'

"I look out at Elaine and then I look back to Annette who's singing to me and I get this resolve in my face. With one hand I grab my uniform and tear it off – it's all Velcro – and I've got a bathing suit underneath. We shot this next part in the big tank at the studios with projection behind us. You cut and there are these big waves with all these guys taking off like it's Makaha; twenty or thirty foot waves. You cut back to Elaine and it's a medium close shot and she's surfing on a wave and suddenly I stand up from the bottom of the frame like I'm surfing right next to her and she looks at me all dreamily.

"All of a sudden, I fall and there's a big splash of water and she looks shocked. Then I stand up again like I may have fallen but I won't be thwarted so easily. She looks at me adoringly again and it all kind of dissolves out of that again."

Perhaps someday Paramount will allow us to see this and other scenes from *Airplane II: The Sequel.*

The Blob (1988)
by Matt Sanborn

It oozed into American theaters on August 5, 1988, proclaiming "Now, terror has no shape," and "Scream now why you can still breathe." A film made at a breakneck pace in two different parts of the country, with a crew of young optimistic upstarts who ignored the immense difficulties of resurrecting a gelatinous monster and produced a minor cinema classic.

The movie is almost a farewell to true film making artistry, being created right before the CGI explosion that would overtake the Hollywood product, pushing out the true craftsmanship of special effects. It is a film that also sent the careers of some of the stars and crew into overdrive.

The Blob.

A remake of a cult classic, different in substance, form, and theme—the beloved child of writer/producer/director Chuck Russell and his writing partner Frank Darabont.

THE BLOB BEGINS FORMING

By 1988 Russell had an enviable career in Hollywood already, having been an assistant director for the 1978 *Just Tell Me You Love Me*, and producing movies such as *The Great American Girl Robbery*, *Dreamscape* (associate producer), *Hell Night* (executive producer), *The Seduction* (executive producer), with the Rodney Dangerfield smash classic *Back to School* (producer and production manager) being a career zenith up to that point. Yet the filmmaker was not satisfied, wanting to call the shots behind the camera.

"I was looking for my first opportunity as a director," remembers Russell. "Both Frank (Darabont) and I have a love for classic monster movies. I needed to find a title to create a break for myself. So I was researching old monster movies and thought (*The Blob*) is a classic, but you could do more with it."

The original would become legend because of its red amorphous monster and for being Steve McQueen's (billed then as Steven McQueen) first lead role. Directed by Irvin S. Yeaworth Jr., it was shot for around $240,000 in Phoenixville, Pennsylvania from July to August 1957 and unleashed onto the America public on September 12, 1958. Upon release, it was considered just one of many of the mass produced sci-fi films of the era, remaining in the public's consciousness due to the future superstardom of its leading man and a famous scene of the Blob squeezing its way through the Colonial Theater. In 2008 it was nominated by the TV Land Awards as "The Best Movie to Watch at the Drive-In."

"As much of a milestone as it was starting Steve McQueen's career, I felt you could do more with the story and the physical effects," says Russell. "I thought there could be more action, more of a sense of humor and *more Blob*."

Frank Darabont was also working his way up through the Hollywood ranks, after starting out as a production assistant in the 1981 *Hell Night* starring Linda Blair, and working as a transportation captain in *The Seduction*. He hit it big as the screenplay writer for *A Nightmare on Elm Street 3: Dream Warriors* in 1987.

Russell and Darabont approached Bob Shea at New Line Cinema about remaking the movie. New Line was riding high on the success of the first two *Nightmare on Elm Street* films, and wanted to stay focused on their money making line, at first turning down the idea for *The Blob* remake. New Line did hire the team to work on *Nightmare on Elm Street III: Dream Warriors*, which Russell would direct, taking the film in a different, effective and more successful direction than its two predecessors. The team took a movie with a budget of close to $4.5 million and turned it into a tremendous financial success, grossing close to $50 million at the American box office.

With the success of *Dream Warriors*, New Line gave the green light to the two men to go ahead and remake the 1958 classic.

Rights for the remake were secured when Russell approached the producer of the original film, Jack Harris. Without much money in the budget, a deal was struck that Harris would become a silent partner and producer.

"We didn't have much money," Russell says. "So we said we can partner with you and you will get the producing credit. It proves one way or another, where there's a will, there's a way."

Jack Harris was present for some of the filming, but according to the film's cinematographer Mark Irwin, he did not have much say in the movie's creation.

"The producer of the original had a lot to say," says Mark Irwin. "Tri-Star said, 'Thanks,' but didn't listen to him very much. It was too bad."

TEAM BLOB BEGINS TO COME TOGETHER

Russell and Darabont then began crafting the script, updating, and setting it in the fictional community of Arborville, a small ski town fallen upon hard economic times. Again the theme of young people trying to convince adults of a supernatural approaching death, (as in the original *Blob* and *Dream Warriors*), is key. As a movie for the times, right in the middle of a new wave of teen sex comedies, there were the dirty gags, double entendre, and underlying sexual cravings not present in the original. There would be far more screen time for titular characters and a far more spectacular ending of fifteen minutes of film, which would push the effects staff and actors to their limit.

The film would also differ from the original as the theme of power transfer is present in the remake. The Shawnee Smith character, Meg Penny, begins as an innocent, virginal cheerleader from an all-American household, and ends up as a gun totting heroine, bent on saving the town with the use of extreme force in the form of a machinegun. Kevin Dillon portrays a young man, Brian Flagg, whose reputation exceeds his reality, becoming a target for harassment by local law enforcement. In the end Flagg is prepared to give up his life in a series of epic deeds of bravery to save the town that disdains him from this extraterrestrial menace, completing his hero-journey.

"Shawnee and Kevin really surprised me at the auditions," Russell remembers. "They seemed like a group of kids who really wanted to save the town."

"Chuck is great," says Dillon.

Shawnee Smith, now a famed scream queen from her role as Amanda Young in the *Saw* series, started her film career as a dancer in the 1982 version of *Annie*, and this would be her first lead role in a major Hollywood production.

Kevin Dillon was already underway to having a fine acting career, having been featured in the TV movie, *No Big Deal* in 1983, scoring a nice part in the 1985 film *Heaven Help Us* as Rooney, and is incredible in a smaller but unforgettable role in Oliver Stone's *Platoon* as Bunny, a near psychotic soldier who enjoys the warrior lifestyle and being in Viet Nam. But he had yet to have a solo lead. In *The Blob* he broke on through to the other side, winning the part and the singular lead male role.

"It was a long time ago," says Dillon, "But I remember I had about five or six auditions. I just kept getting callbacks. And I got the part. I remember Chuck saying, 'I'd love it if you hit the gym a little bit. Get in better shape. Hit the gym and get a little bulkier.' I don't think I ever did. I probably should have hit the gym a little bit," he says laughing.

The director also requested another change in the actor.

"He wanted me to grow my hair out. I didn't have enough time. He liked the long hair thing, you know. And that's why we went with those awful extensions that we got on the show."

Although Dillon laughs about his wig, the style was certainly that of the late 1980s.

"It makes it look a little bit dated. It's kinda funny. It's got a mullet vibe about it. A friend of mine auditioned for it, and he had long hair. Chuck said, 'Man, I wish you had hair like (him).' I got the job, but (he) had long straight black hair."

Upon winning the role, Dillon immediately understood to whom he would be compared.

"I'm a big Steve McQueen fan, man," he says. "Big time. I also liked the Triumph for the motorcycle. Steve McQueen was a big Triumph guy. I looked at it as a big honor to redo a movie that Steve McQueen once did. If you watch the original *Blob*, it wasn't a great movie," adding with a laugh, "it was pretty rough."

Russell also brought in veteran cinematographer Mark Irwin, who had filmed the visionary David Cronenberg movies *The Fly*, *Scanners*, and the dystopian classic *Videodrome*.

"This was the first film I had shot in '88," recalls Irwin. "The previous year I had shot *The Fly*, and the remake mentality was very prevalent at the time. I met with Chuck and he liked what I did. *The Fly* was a very indoor film, where *The Blob* was a very outdoor kind of film."

Hoyt Yeatman of Dream Quest Images was brought in as the visual effects supervisor, having worked with Russell on *Dream Warriors* as the special video effects supervisor.

"It posed the challenge of not only the creature itself," says Yeatman, "but the amount of destruction they wanted to show."

Donovan Leitch, son of Sixties pop musician Donovan ("Mellow Yellow") was cast as Paul Taylor, Candy Clark as waitress Fran Hewitt, the incredible Del Weeks as the Reverend Meeker, legendary Jack Nance was brought in for a small part as a doctor, Paul McCrane as Deputy Bill Briggs and Jeffery DeMunn was hired later to play the part of Sheriff Herb Geller.

"They had another actor for the part," recalls DeMunn. "Things didn't work out so well, so it was a last minute deal. These were pre-computer days really, and they couldn't even get a script to me. I just said, 'Sure.' I knew the original and I read the script on the plane there. I said, 'Let's go, let's see.'"

To DeMunn the part at the time was just another gig for a working actor.

"I was just doing the next job," he says. "The first one was a classic. I liked the idea, so I went out there."

There being Abbeville, Louisiana.

THE BLOB EMERGES ON ABBEVILLE

Abbeville, Louisiana is a small town of 5.7 square miles whose population was less than 12,000 and shrinking at the time due to the economy. It houses vintage American architecture within many of its buildings. During the Reagan era some of the residents had become wealthy due to the discovery of crude oil reserves on their properties, while others had to leave town to find employment – a town practically personifying the economic state of the 1980s.

The team of close to 150 members showed up in early January 1988 to prepare for a January 12 kick off, with most everybody staying at a Travelodge.

Chuck Russell: "We were shooting in the winter, and the place was reasonably warm. It was the perfect small town to shoot. It had classic American architecture, and I wanted to make a classic American horror film. The look of the place was just right... There were people there that hunted alligators. There were big oyster beds. I had an incredible time there."

Although the buildings were perfect for what Russell was looking for, the flora and fauna presented a completely different problem for the film crew.

Mark Irwin: "The streets were literally paved with oyster shells. Chuck wanted it to look like a classic New England town, but there were problems. We had to remove all the Spanish moss from the area and see what we could do."

Although accommodating, the townsfolk did not allow Russell to chop down a large oak tree in front of the courthouse, remembers Hoyt Yeatman. Overall, the people of the town opened their stores and arms to the Hollywood cast, crew and cash.

Hoyt Yeatman: "We pretty much got the run of the place. It is amazing when you go out in the boonies where they don't see much of the film business—they are infatuated with Hollywood, unlike (in California) where no one wants you to park and hates movie crews. We were the entertainment. There were literally hundreds of people who came out to see the shooting, especially at night."

The leading man was certainly treated as a first class citizen.

Kevin Dillon: "We went down to Abbeville, and they actually deputized me. So when you're in the town of Abbeville, I want you on your best behavior... It was a little town, but I loved Abbeville."

Kat Fenton, who was a makeup artist on the set, remembers the town fondly: "The people bent over backwards for us. The movie brought in a cash flow."

Jeffery DeMunn: "It was an interesting, tiny little town. It had (economically) collapsed. They were reliant on oil. There was a lot of need of cash there. But we put carpenters to work. We put electricians to work."

Some of the people were also very interested in meeting their guests.

Jeffery DeMunn: "I remember I got to know some of the folks locally. A few were millionaires from oil and gas. They owned marsh-land you could buy for next to nothing and suddenly they were millionaires. One guy picked me up at 9 a.m. to show me the real Louisiana coast and took me to his uncle's place and to hunt nutria."

Nutria, also known as coypu, being a large and semi-aquatic rodent, brought into America by fur ranchers.

DeMunn: "They are the world's largest rat, and were introduced there by mistake. They got loose and started destroying root systems. So we went out in airboats to hunt these giant rats. We hunted them and then went back to this one guy's house. He had just built this big house and it had no furniture in it. It's 9 a.m. and they're pushing beers on me. By 11 a.m. I had to go back to the hotel and go to bed. I had a 6:00 p.m. shoot."

The filming was done mostly at night, turning the biological clocks around for most everybody.

Chuck Russell: "You would wake up at 3 p.m., have some oysters and coffee, and go to work. It was good."

The locals also hosted dances and hunts for other members as well.

Kat Fenton: "It was beautiful there. It wasn't muggy or humid. The people were very nice. The food was fabulous."

Dillon: "They had entertainment every night. All kinds of New Orleans kind of vibe. All kinds of Creole cooking. They had the washboard going. It was a real Louisiana town."

And on days off people like Dillon and Fenton would go to the Big Easy for more fun.

Dillon: "Every chance we got we went to New Orleans and partied there. It was fun, man. It was fun on weekends, running into New Orleans. Having a good old time. But they know how to party right there in Abbeville as well. It was a blast, absolutely a blast. It was fun and I had a great time."

As mild as the days were, the temperatures dropped as the sun set, making it difficult to shoot scenes that were supposed to be during warmer weather.

Mark Irwin: "There was a Catch 22. It was supposed to be a hot summer night, and they went about as far south as they could go. It looked very New Englandish, but it was thirty three degrees every night. The actors were chewing on ice cubes to make sure their breath didn't show."

THE BIRTHING OF THE BLOB

It was supposed to be a small job for young makeup artist Tony Gardner.

"I was only supposed to do a couple of minor effects," he recalls.

However, once production started, the young makeup artist was asked to take on the responsibility of heading the entire special effects team.

"At the time, I was 24 and this was the first big *anything* I had ever done," says Gardner.

On the other side of the studio, the Blob side, Lyle Conway was hired to create the titular character.

"They wanted the Blob to be a stand-alone character," says Gardner. "(Lyle) had done Audrey for (the remake of) *Little Shoppe of Horrors*."

"Lyle was taking on a task never done before," adds Chuck Russell. "It had never been done on that scale. The Blob had to be as a full scale physical effect. It was too much."

The director gave the film team a firm directive: The Blob must be a living, breathing threat.

A warehouse studio for the effects was set up off of Hollywood Boulevard with two crews working side by side, with a piece of tape on the studio floor separating the personal effects and Blob effects side.

"Our shop was located right in downtown Hollywood," recalls Evan Brainard, an effects artist on the film. "It was very entertaining and fun, because after work we would often end up at a restaurant, bar, or movie together. There might've been from three to fifteen people all together."

The crew would need to pull together as new answers had to be created to produce the never-done-before effects for the film. Without the use of CGI, everything would have to be done by hand.

"I was learning at the time. This was the first time I had a giant crew. It was so much fun. We were so stupid," says Gardner.

Under the guidance of the young Gardner, a youthful, joyous atmosphere took over the overworked studio members. To relieve some of the fatigue and tension Gardner held theme days during the work week.

"On my side of the shop we would have vampire day, where everyone dressed up like a vampire. We had black and white day. Cowboy day. Tie day. It was just the goofiest group of people. We were dead tired all the time."

Due to the overwhelming amount of work, the two sides of the studio, one doing the Blob and one doing the other visual effects, merged.

"There was a point about half way through the show that the two teams had to become one," says Russell. "That's one thing I had to be ready for as a director; if something doesn't work in the game plan."

The effects teams merged without ego clashing or toe stepping.

Evan Brainard: "It was a different time, and certainly a director who appreciated working with practical effects."

The Blob side of the shop was at a bit of a disadvantage, working to produce a monster which had never been done in this fashion, as well as having very little lead time for research and development. Testing would only resume once primary shooting had begun; many Blob effects would have to be thought out on the fly.

Conway fashioned as many tricks as he could, using silicon to create the see-through gelatinous appearance of the creature. The viscosity of the being would create its movement.

"To get it to drip they used methyl cellulose," says Mark Irwin. "It is a food additive from wood pulp."

The compound is derived from cellulose, and comes in a thick white powder which dissolves in hot water, forming a clear gel. It is also used as a treatment for constipation, a thickener for fast food milkshakes, as a glue, to create fake tears or sweat, a lubricant, and as a vegetarian alternative in the making of food capsules.

Mark Irwin: "The next time you have a milkshake, think of the Blob."

"I've been drinking the Blob all this time," jokes Kevin Dillon upon hearing this news.

The task of filming this slimy beast was squarely laid in the capable hands of Irwin.

"The Blob itself was created in so many fashions," he says. "Some of it was with liquids. Some of it was puppeted. It had to be lit in a different way to be luminous… It was slimy. It was unbelievably slippery, like a slip, fall and break a hip kind of thing. And it was difficult to work around."

The talented and experienced Irwin and team were able to work through it without incident.

"The Blob was really difficult for Lyle to make," says Yeatman, "because of its organic nature. It was very late in the game when we got the Blob working. It was crazy when you look at it. It was almost like tie-died silk and they injected into it this goopy methyl cellulose. It's an inert gooey substance. This sack weighed hundreds of pounds. And to puppet it, we had puppeteers under the table kinda pushing and prodding it. And in some instances there was a puppeteer inside the thing with a scuba regulator in his mouth so he could writhe around in this thing. It was very much an organic process."

While working with the methyl cellulose, the team found out something else about the compound.

"The odd thing about it," adds Yeatman, "that I never knew it would do, was destroy all the asphalt around our building. It would expand and contract with the temperature and it eventually destroyed all the tarmac around the building. We had to repave afterwards. So stuff you can eat, also can take out stuff."

When life sized parts of the Blob were not in use, things were scaled down, as an 80'x30' model of the town of Abbeville was then constructed for the miniature scenes. When certain scenes were filmed, paths and spaces were cut into the bottom so the Blob could be manipulated from below by puppeteers.

"We built very large sections of the town that we would destroy," recalls Hoyt Yeatman.

Every morning the monster was needed, the team would mix the powder into gallons of water, and then with large gauge syringes, inject it into the painted silk sack, which had a waffle pattern on it. The process took several hours every day before shooting could begin. Then puppeteers in rain coats would go beneath cut areas of the miniatures table and puppeteer the silk bundle of methyl cellulose. The Blob was then shot at 96 frames-a-second to produce the proper speed needed for matching it with the 24 frames-a-second of the live action.

"It was always oozing outside the silk," remembers Yeatman. "That's what gave it its kind of appearance. It was constantly being refilled and replaced. So if you were doing a scene where the Blob came into contact with something, you had to clean everything. It was a very messy, thankless job."

A thankless job which would continue as the primary shooting began, due to the amount of problems the title character caused. As the Blob team tried to find a way to make the creature work, other effects were worked out before heading to the first shooting destination in Abbeville, Louisiana. One of these effects being the five and a half hour set up for the burn makeup on legendary improv comedian, teacher and actor Del Close.

"Del was great," Tony remembers.

DEL CLOSE AND JACK NANCE

As the film helped propel further the careers of Shawnee Smith, Tony Gardner and Kevin Dillon, it also became a near swan song for two of the all-time great quirky character actors of their time. The first actor was Jack Nance, who came to underground cinema legend status as Henry Spencer in David Lynch's *Eraserhead*. He showed great promise in that film, and stood out in other Lynch vehicles *Blue Velvet* and *Twin Peaks*, yet did not work as steadily as his talent should have allowed. A troubled yet greatly gifted actor, the death of Nance is one of great debate. The day before his death, two days before the beginning of 1997, he claimed to have been in a fist fight with two men whom he boasted to have verbally disparaged near Winchell's Doughnut Shop near his apartment in South Pasadena, California. He was sporting a large bruise under his eye and was complaining of a headache after the alleged event. He was found on December 30th dead in his bathroom. It is possible there was no fight and the actor simply fell when drunk and hit his head, causing the bruise. His cause of death was subdural hematoma, which can be caused by a blow or blows to the head. He was 53 years old.

Nance played the town's doctor and one of the Blob's first victims.

"Jack was very quiet," remembers Tony Gardner. "We really didn't get to talk to him much, and I regret that."

The director appreciated the talent and depth which Nance brought to the role.

"He was another interesting, eerie kind of guy," Russell says. "He was a method actor and he wanted to know everything about his scene and his role... Nance was a real plus."

The other actor portrayed one of the most memorable characters in *The Blob* - Reverend Meeker, the apocalyptic preacher who would be burnt terribly in the mayhem the monster brings to town, was Del Close - a legend in the Chicago improv and theater scene.

"He was the king of improv comedy in Chicago," says Jeffery DeMunn. "When he died he left his skull to a theater in Chicago to display and use in Hamlet. An evening with him was fabulous."

Chuck Russell laughs when hearing about his skull donation: "It sounds like him."

Controversy arose after the actor's March 4th, 1999 death, as a skull was eventually delivered to the Goodman Theatre in Chicago, only to be discovered later that it was not Close's brain cover.

Del was on the set of *Saturday Night Live* in its nascent days coaching the Not Ready for Prime Time Players including his

improv students John Belushi, Gilda Radner and Dan Aykroyd. He spent many years in the Second City coaching talent such as John Candy, Chris Farley, Tina Fey, Wavy Gravy, Bill Murray Bob Odenkirk, Harold Ramis and George Wendt.

Due to the makeup effects he would have to wear later in the film Close had to keep his hair long. He also dropped over 30 pounds for the role. Tony Gardner's crew brought him in for makeup tests for the burn makeup he would have to wear. After fitting the prosthetics on the actor, the team could not believe what followed.

"He went onto this platform in the shop in character of a burn guy. He did like twenty minutes of being a burn victim. You can't ask for anything better when gluing stuff to his face. He was a nice, nice man."

Chuck Russell also praises the actor for his contributions.

"Nobody could have played the part of the reverend like Del. He was the heart of the Chicago theater and a wonderful teacher. He could go to another level if you had time to go to another level."

But for the production, there would be very little time.

THE BLOB GETS A BIT STICKY

On January 12, primary filming commenced at an intense pace.

"It was one of those down and dirty shoots," says Kat Fenton, a key makeup artist on the film, (who is credited as Kathryn Miles Kelly).

With the youth of the cast and crew, the production did not seem to notice or care the cramped timeframe they were up against.

"Chuck was so enthusiastic," says Tony Gardner. "The actors were so committed. Everyone was trying. The shooting schedule was so unrealistic."

"It was rough," remembers Kevin Dillon. "We shot some in Abbeville and some here in L.A. We shot a lot of it right here in Griffith Park (in Los Angeles). It was cold at night and most of the shoot was at night. There was a straight month where I hardly saw any daylight. You sleep all day and you do it again. It was rough and it beat you up after a while."

Due to a short filming timeframe and limited financial resources, every moment of shooting was vital.

"We had very little time and money. I had to go in with this mind set," says Russell. "This was down and dirty guerrilla film making. I had to give it the production values of a feature film. We had to use our wits. We were forced into creative solutions. It was do or die every day."

The monster had never been done on that level and without CGI technology evolved to the level it needed to be, everything had to be done by hand with either real size parts of the creature or miniatures. The time consuming effects were coupled with intense physical performances, with some of them involving complicated stunts, working with children, and acting when the monster is not present in front of the talent.

"We were limited," says Russell. "The effects are uneven. We bit off a bit more than we could chew. But it is in the spirit of great indie horror."

There were three extremely challenging scenes in a film of challenging scenes. One being the amazing ending where the Blob squares off against the military and townspeople, requiring proper timing, shooting, and explosions, plus some difficult effects. The second is the famous "Phone Booth Death" where both Sherriff

Herb Geller and Candy Clark are destroyed by the gelatinous invader, one inside and one outside the booth. The third is the first appearance of the Blob in the local hospital.

The Hospital Massacre

Dripping from the walls and ceiling the Blob makes its spectacular first appearance in the film, and Tony Gardner and crew were the ones responsible for making it memorable.

"(Chuck Russell) said to me, let's shoot the first attack at the end of the schedule," says Gardner. "He said, 'It really needs to sell.' We were able to focus on the first Blob scene. Everything else was run and gun, but the first scene we could take our time and storyboard it. We knew what was in Chuck's head."

Russell felt the first appearance of the monster was so important that more film was shot for its grand entrance even as the editing phase of the production had begun. The Blob appears out of nowhere at first, so the director along with the effects team came up with a preamble to tease the coming of the creeping, slimy mess.

Tony Gardner: "While Chuck was editing he said, 'We need a lead up scene to make this scary.' We came up with the idea of it moving under the blanket but you still don't see it. We shot it the last week. It really was a collaborative effort across the board."

This scene where the creature takes its first two victims, Paul Taylor (Donovan Leitch) and the doctor (Jack Nance), is creepy and slow, with Shawnee Smith selling very well for the bubbling terror which invades her safe world view. First the monster percolates up under the sheets of the infected Paul, then is exposed by the Doctor. The Blob then takes hold of the hapless teen's body and begins dissolving it.

"We sculpted a giant clay version around Donovan," says Gardner. "We then took a 'Blob quilt' and moved it over things. We were able to figure cool stuff out."

Paul Taylor who brags early in the film his wish to deflower his virginal accompaniment (Meg) plays into one of the predominant undercurrents of horror films of the conservative 1980s – that all those participating or wishing for casual sex will find an untimely and gruesome demise. This undercurrent flows through almost the entire *Friday the 13th* series, some of the *Nightmare on Elm Street* films, and scores of other horror flicks in the Reagan/burgeoning AIDS era.

After escaping infected from his bed, the dying Paul stumbles his way into the doctor's office where Meg watches helplessly as her date for the night turns to ooze, his arm melting before her eyes.

Gardner is bothered to this day by the scene which was shot low, briefly revealing a hole in the floor where the performers arm can be seen sliding down into and out of view. It is a brief glimpse of how the trick was done, and if one is not looking, one will miss it.

The Phone Booth Encasement

In perhaps the movie's most famous scene, terrified waitress Candy Clark flees her restaurant, entering a phone booth desperate to summon help from an unknown horror she can yet only sense. With the phone line dead, she turns to see that her mindless pursuer has encased what has become her glass execution chamber. Screaming frantically as the creature tightens its grip, the face of the dissolving Sherriff Herb Geller presses against the glass, a harbinger for her upcoming and horrific fate.

This effect was created by using a water tank and having the exterior scenery slide by, creating a rolling effect. Mechanics were put inside a life cast face mask of Jeffery DeMunn distorting the face, giving the appearance something is trying to burst through his skull.

"We used silks and strange fabrics so it looked like dissolved tissue," reveals Gardner. "In the water it moved nicely. The pieces just came streaming off."

The scene effectively created the vision of what the effects master wanted to present on the screen.

"In my mind," says Gardner, "the Blob was a giant stomach or lye pit. Everything is collapsing into itself. It looks like things are dissolving in water. Like when you drop those Easter egg tablets into water and you have those color streams that disappear. That's what I thought it would look like."

The shot is overhead and Candy is screaming as the Blob slithers by, a silky material in a tank free moving and unyielding. Finally the creature takes hold and everything collapses into a miasma of color and viscera like never seen before on screen. A triumph of practical special effects, done with water and silks.

"There was kind of a water tank with a shell around it," says Mark Irwin, "so when the Blob descended, it would appear flush to the wall, or it would have sluiced away. Jeffery DeMunn's face was puppeted. It was a lot of fun. It was almost like live theater. It was like a live show."

The Climactic Battle

The final fifteen minutes is an action driven, frenetic combination of panic, horror and preternatural violence. Scientists, government officials, scared teens, town folks, soldiers, and one very bizarre reverend scatter everywhere on the streets and mass panic takes hold. Guns are pointed at one another; the Blob is the centerpiece in this chaos. This race to the finish is laced potently with violence, explosions, stunts and special effects.

"The most difficult thing was the whole ending with Shawnee as a cheerleader with an automatic weapon on a snow truck," recalls the director. "We had hired a CGI team but it was not possible to do organic looking CGI at the time."

The climax on the movie rested on the shoulders of Gardner and his team. The result was quite acceptable to the director: "The film had surprisingly good effects. We did have to reconfigure how the Blob was killed. The technology just wasn't there and we had to go back to miniatures."

One of the memorable effects of the finale is the falling apart of a soldier.

"He was a triple amputee," says Tony Gardner. "He partially dissolves in the road. We used spandexes, bags of slime, and dressed it up with tendrils and slime. The same materials worked outside and in the water as well."

There are many miniatures used in this scene, but up close, the Blob still had to be of actual substance. The monster itself became an interesting conglomeration of materials.

Tony Gardner: "We made a quilt out of transparent silk and injected it with silicon caulking. Everything was foam latex. We had to paint it to look translucent, because at the time there was not translucent latex."

The Blob also had its own problems after a certain size.

Gardner remembers, "We were injecting it with window-like caulking to shape things. It would dry but keep its shape and we could control it to a certain size. We used miniatures for some scenes, because at a certain size, it would become unwieldy."

Any time there was destruction of the town, the miniature sets were used.

Hoyt Yeatman: "This is all photographically done. We didn't have all the paint out tools. Any time there was physical reaction, any time the Blob had to come into contact, then miniatures were used. These were very, very large tabletops that were built and lit under very high levels of light, and then shot under high speed photography to blend the two (live and miniature shots) together."

Despite the effects team working on its feet and trying to come up with answers to problems that had never been presented to them before, the filming continued at a furious pace.

"We either had to shoot it or rewrite it," remarks the director.

Tension builds as the monster begins to take hold of the town and the military is brought in to deal with the escalating situation. Helicopters and cars chase the young couple of Penny and Flagg on the young man's motorcycle. This high action scene would not have been quite as remarkable had it not been filmed a few miles away from where the tragic *Twilight Zone* movie helicopter scene had been filmed in the early 1980s.

"We were well aware of (the *Twilight Zone* accident), and we pulled it off," Irwin says. "It was the ethos that you could do it."

Although the film had the spirit of a true independent film, the crew had 4-5 cameras for most shots, and were able to take their time for set up. Chuck Russell was the driving force, and took a personal affinity to the creature.

"He would always say, 'My Blob,'" says Irwin. "Chuck had a very strong take on it. He was very proprietary."

"Chuck knew what he wanted," says Dillon. "We were good buddies. I thought he was a great guy. By the end of the shoot we were tight. He has an intensity about him as well. He knew what he wanted and he wanted it delivered. He could get a little intense at times, but I loved that. You want to see that."

Russell worked diligently to create the proper look for the film as well.

"This is where Chuck really showed me how dedicated he was," remembers the cinematographer. "There were not enough pine trees in the area for the shot we were doing. So he shelled out to have them cut down from northern California, trucked in, then augured and planted."

More shooting was done after the three weeks in Abbeville, at locations in and around Los Angeles, such as Griffith Park.

"I remember seventeen weeks of night shooting," says Irwin.

"It was a fun movie to work on," says Dillon. "It was a lot of work. I made some good friends… It was a tough shoot, man. Such a tough shoot. Doing all those night scenes and freezing."

DELETED SCENES

Two scenes were shot for the film that never made it to the final cut. Near the end as Brian is driving his motorcycle with Meg on the back through the sewers of town, trying to outrun the government officials, they are startled as the beast appears in front of them as they head full throttle toward its direction.

Kevin Dillon did most of his own riding for the movie.

"I've always loved bikes. I'm pretty good on them," he says. "I did all my own riding except for the stunts."

Dillon is especially fond of the Triumph motorcycle used in the film.

"It had to be a Triumph. Got to be a tougher thing for Brian to have. It gives him a harder edge."

An early scene in the film shows Flagg jumping a gorge where a bridge has collapsed. Fortunately for his health, Dillon did not attempt the exceptionally dangerous stunt the director wanted as a breathtaking visual helping to build towards the climax of the film.

The original script called for a grand, almost comical effect to occur. The fleeing couple was to encounter the aggressive slime in front of them. With no time to turn, and crashing into or hitting the beast, spelling a terrible and painful demise, Flagg takes his bike and does the old cycle-atronic trick by looping over the beast in a complete 360 degree stunt, moving above the creature by circling the pipe and avoiding a terrible fate.

Tony Gardner: "We built a dummy of Shawnee Smith hugging Kevin Dillon on the motorcycle, squinting with her eyes closed. A stunt man was going to spin in the tunnel and they were going to comp in the Blob later with CGI so he loops over it. They built a giant section of the tunnel, but they never got it right."

Kevin Dillon: "There was a crazy stunt where they tried to do a flip inside the tunnel... It was a crazy stunt. They got these guys from the 'Sphere of Death,' and they drive around circles. They had these guys try it, but it was on the move. So these guys drove towards the Blob and then flip around. It was insane. Crazy stunts."

Unfortunately due to gravity, the stunt could not be perfected, and the scene was eventually scrapped.

A second scene which was never created was to kick off the climax. Brian Flagg has delivered the snow producing truck to the front of the church where many of the town people have gone for refuge from the Blob. Instead of slowly freeing himself in a faux-climax as seen in the film, the Kevin Dillon character was instead to be sucked into a manhole and down into the sewers. Immersed into the murky waters the young man struggles to get to the surface when the body and grossly distorted face of the doctor floats by, corroded and terrifying.

Tony Gardner: "We built a water tank. You were going to see the doctor float by. The Blob was bigger and stronger now and dissolving things at a faster rate. The doctor's face was distorted and his mouth was about one and a half feet long. Another face was stretched out and cast in translucent iridescence. It was very surreal. The day we were supposed to shoot it, there was a crack in the tank, so we couldn't shoot it."

THE BLOB SLIDES INTO THE SUNSET

Reviews of the film were mixed. Richard Harrington of the *Washington Post* wrote a review for the August 5, 1988 edition complaining that it was one of many recent 1950s remakes: "The effects start regressing until, at film's end, they have much of the same chintzy 'faked' look as the original." And stating that no more remakes were needed: "What's next? How about a remake of the original *Blob's* frequent double-bill partner, *I Married a Monster From Outer Space?* Or *It Conquered the World?* Or *The Alligator People?* The possibilities are endless ... unfortunately."

However, the *New York Times'* Janet Maslin was far kinder about the effects in her August 5, 1988 review: "The Blob itself is the most impressive cast member, a genuinely clever creation that's at least as versatile as it is disgusting." And stating: "Modern technology has yielded at least one definite advance in the last 30 years: a better Blob."

Despite some reviews and the fascinating posters and intriguing trailers, the film failed to become a huge box office success. Nonetheless, it is still a fan favorite, and an Eighties cult classic.

"I had a feeling about it," says Kevin Dillon. "I felt it had a cult vibe-ish. Like the original."

And the actor still remembers the movie fondly.

"I'm proud of it," says Dillon. "I've got some pride for *The Blob* for sure. Especially with the limited technology we had back then... It's cool (people are) still talking about it."

"It developed a life of its own," muses Jeffery DeMunn. "It deserved to have some of that. We were working hard day and night. It's a good film."

And although the film is somewhat of a straight "popcorn movie," there is more behind the slime and action.

"I don't know if it a social commentary about AIDS or where the feminist movement was at the time," says Mark Irwin. "But the drive-in roots were kept. I think Chuck succeeded. I was happy to embrace it."

Irwin also compares it to other films he has worked on.

"For me, when you are viewing films and you break it down as either an FM or an AM film. *The Blob* was an AM film, where *Videodrome* was an FM film."

"It still gets laughs and scares at the right places," says Russell. "Horror fans are very consistent folks."

References

www.imdb.com

www.tvland.com

www.wikipedia.com

http://www.lynchnet.com/absent/nancepre.html

Skullduggery, The New Yorker, October 9, 20006

"Not even close: Skull not that of improv legend," *Chicago Tribune News*, October 5, 2006

Brottman, Mikita, *Hollywood Hex, Death and Destiny in the Dream Factory*, Creation Books,1999

"The Blob," Richard Harrington, *The Washington Post*, August 5, 1988

"'The Blob,' Modernized," *The New York Times*, August 5, 1988

976 Evil II:
The Astral Factor
by Mike White

In 1982, Eddie Murphy threatened to boil a live lobster on *Saturday Night Live* unless he was saved via a call-in campaign. Viewers could vote to save or boil "Larry the Lobster" via two different 1-900 phone numbers. Though premium rate telephone numbers had been in existence since 1971, it was the success of the *Saturday Night Live* skit that put them into the public consciousness. Late night television in the '80s and early '90s became lousy with ads for phone sex, psychics, and celebrities ("Dial 1-900-909-TONE to talk to Tone Loc!").

Even Saturday morning cartoons weren't safe from 1-900 and 976 advertisements. Children could call and hear Santa tell them a story or talk to their favorite storybook character and nerds could vote to save the Boy Wonder, Robin, from death! The popularity of these numbers diminished in the wake of the Internet.

Never a genre to shy away from a trend, Robert Englund's 1988 film *976-EVIL* featured a demonic dial-up where a throaty Robert Picardo would offer up unlimited power to callers. Of course, the price for their newfound ability came at price higher than $2.99 for the first minute and $2.00 for every minute after that. Instead, it cost them their souls.

Englund's film (his sole feature directorial effort until 2008's *Killer Pad*) featured a script by Rhet Topham (*Trick or Treat*) and Brian Helgeland (*L.A. Confidential, Payback*) and stars Patrick O'Bryan as Leonard "Spike" Johnson who lives across the street from his wacky Aunt Lucky (Sandy Dennis) and nerdy, voyeuristic cousin Hoax (Stephen Geoffreys). Much like the Chester and Spike characters of the Warner Bros. cartoons, Hoax is a hanger on to Spike. However, when he learns of the 976-EVIL hotline, Hoax begins to exact revenge on those who have wronged him.

Geoffreys's Hoax was not too far removed from his role in *Fright Night* while his seemingly amorous regard for Spike would foreshadow Geoffreys's later roles in films like *Leather After Midnight* and *Hunk Hotel*.

Produced by Cinetel films and distributed by New Line Cinema (the "House that Freddy Built"), the film fared well at the box office and did great business as a video store staple. It's not surprising that a sequel would follow.

"I'm not going to be able to tell exactly why we got to do the sequel other than [Cinetel] did the first one," recalls producer Catalaine "Cat" Knell. Founded in 1980 by Paul Hertzberg and Lisa M. Hansen as Chicago Teleproductions, Cinetel Films hit their stride with the video store boom of the '80s. From 1986 onward they've produced and/or distributed an average of six films a year (and they're still going strong today).

Knell continues, "It was sort of the heyday of the foreign market in home video. It was a time that those of us who participated in it wish that it would visit us again. But at that time, independent filmmaking was very easy to finance because you could basically lay out the domestic and we had a couple of output deals with New Line and Tri-Star, at the time, which aren't in existence anymore. So they would buy the domestic rights and then send it to all the set ups so that it made its money by selling to foreign territories, and selling in all the different formats for TV, film. But most of our movies would go straight to video which in home entertainment was a money maker at that point. Because, as today, theatrical is basically advertising for the afterlife of a film in TV and video."

Screenwriter Eric Anjou recalls, "Cinetel had the bank to make money. Part of that bank was predicated on the fact that they had to get certain genre elements that were necessary for financing and there were certain cast elements, talent elements. A lot of times they would have a script that was in kind of like decent shape, but they really couldn't send it out. They wanted to get a couple of really cool actors involved so they ended up bringing me in to kind of do a rewrite so the script was a little bit sharper so they could get some of the talent they wanted to cast."

"When you're an independent and you're not working within the studio, you need to find talented people who don't have agents yet, and so you are much more open to looking for the talent when nobody else is," says Knell. "Anybody can find somebody talented after they've been discovered but who are the people that do the discovering? And that's why these small places like Cinetel and Roger Corman and all those entities that are no longer in existence work with amazing talents because we are the ones who took the chance and gave them their first film and allowed them to screw up if they were gonna screw up. But in our cases, if you look at our movies, the writers on our movies are pretty phenomenal and I would say forty percent have gone off and had major careers. Other ones have had big careers in the independent world; they've never gone over to the hundred million dollar team, but they still had pretty good careers. Cinetel paid Quentin [Tarantino] his first fee and had him write on a movie called *Past Midnight.* And he got the movie a green light with his past but then we got into some complications with the Writer's Guild arbitration so, in fact, I shared my producing credit with Quentin on that one."

The first *976-EVIL* film was a financial gold mine so a sequel was a no-brainer. Why, however, did it take three years before the second film came out? Says Knell, "People wanted to do it right away because that meant more money for us but it wasn't like you had to wait. You can do sequels whenever. At a certain point you call it a remake. If you wait ten years, it becomes a remake. The first one made a ton of money so the second one should have been real easy. What you normally did was you made the second film or the third film for half or one third the budget of the first one and you were pretty much counting on the title to get it off the shelves.

"*976-EVIL* was very early in my tenure at Cintel, so at that point, this was a movie that had already been made and I was the Vice President of Creative and it was my job to handle the script writing and handle the creative aspect of it. "

Says Anjou, "I can't remember how I got introduced to [Cinetel], but it was that time where these low budget genre pictures were getting a lot of credence because you could do pre-sales overseas to get bonafide markets for this product, and so I hooked up with Cinetel and I started rewriting scripts for them. And *976-EVIL 2* is one of the scripts that I rewrote for Cinetel. There had been an original, I guess there was a *976-EVIL* one, and they wanted to riff off that and do a two and so I got involved somewhere in that trajectory.

"I think that there's no way to excel at anything in life unless you commit to it seriously and Cinetel was a company, you can laugh at a company like that, but then you look at the Jonathan Demmes and the Martin Scorseses and the wonderful filmmakers that cut their teeth for that guy and Cinetel was a like opportunity for people that were serious. They had bank, they were making money, they were genre pictures, but if you could distinguish yourself as someone of note within the genre, as a craftsman, then there was kind of like a way to move forward. So at the time I was doing three things at once: I was working at a restaurant in Beverly Hills, I was writing the first or second or third draft of a spec screenplay, and I was working with Cintel with the idea that if they liked my work and I could come up with a good spec project, that I'd get a shot to direct for them. So that's definitely something that I took seriously. "

Anjou was not the original writer of *976-EVIL 2*. That was Rick Glassman. Says director Jim Wynorski, "He wrote a script that got thrown out. I had no idea, I wasn't involved with it. But a lot of the script had to be re-written to accommodate what Cinetel wanted."

Anjou adds, "I came into film from more of a 'literary intellectual' point of view, you know. You want to make *The Godfather*, you want to make *Chinatown*, you want to make films that you think matter, but you don't become a brain surgeon right away."

Wynorski continues, "I can't remember the exact process of what it took to construct *976-EVIL 2*, but there was a general process working with Cinetel and they had the original writer's draft and this was the movie they were planning on making. It was a genre picture, and I guess they had certain market places overseas taken care of and now it was getting the right kind of actors that they felt were financeable, given the budget. So I probably did a first draft, if I remember the basic Cinetel template, to keep it structurally intact, so I didn't really change the first, second, third act trajectory of the piece, I just basically rewrote scenes, sharpened up dialogue, that kind of stuff. "

"Now Jim Wynorski has made many, many, many, many movies with Cinetel," says Knell. "But I'm not really clear about that relationship with Paul Herzberg. He was very good friends with the people he made the movies with and remained friends. He would socialize with them and work with them and he and Jim Wynorski were terrific friends. For whatever reason, he was amazingly creative, he just had no goals. His goal was to do what he did and he did it well."

Anjou continues, "As Jim Wynorski came on board to direct—you know Jim's a wonderful, creative, energetic guy, but he's not necessarily a writer, so at a certain point in the process they brought me on to work directly with Jim who had his own ideas about what made movies like this work and what he felt he needed to make *976-EVIL II* successful. I had a meeting with him, I think I met with him at the Cinetel office originally, and then he said, 'Come over to my place in the valley and we'll start working on the script together,' and his den is littered with posters of all the B-movies he directed, and on a refrigerator it's just festooned with 8x10 glossies of strippers. You know, 'Dear Jim, thanks for all the help with my career,' kind of stuff. So you never knew how his cake was iced.

"There's a pecking order in how these smaller genre movies get made. And so it was a real education working with Cinetel and also working with Jim because they took these movies, it's easy for one to be an 'intellectual' and look down on these kind of films, but guys like Jim take them really, really seriously. They want to have fun, they want to get laid (that's definitely part of their agenda), but they also really know certain genre elements that make these movies work. And so it was really fun working with him because as well as wanting to get laid, he actually took the craft of wanting to make the movie very seriously.

"There are certain movements in cinematic history and the American New Wave, these guys like the Spielbergs and the Scorceses and the Paul Schraders, they came out of the time where they went to film school so they were greatly affected by foreign films, French New Wave stuff, and they had the opportunity little by little to both number one, forge their own work as writers and number two, there was a time in Hollywood when the seams were cracking and there were opportunities for young filmmakers to get their feet wet. Not all of them made great movies to begin with, but a lot of guys started with Corman. So I saw this as an opportunity in a time revisited not quite 25 years later. These guys are making movies. They're making movies that are selling and they're remaking this movie again and again and again so what a wonderful time to learn as a filmmaker. Because you're not gonna go out and make *The Godfather*, or *8 ½* or *Chinatown* first time out of the gate. So I looked at it as this very exciting exercise to be in the business, to be with people that were making movies, to be with people like Jim that were passionate and intentioned about the kind of stuff that he was trying to get done. So it's fun working with people who love what they do, especially in Jim's case with a lot of strippers around.

"It's fun but everything is a challenge, so you have to figure out like Jim is trying to do with the direction, I'm trying to do with the script. You don't want anyone to laugh at your work. At whatever level you're working, you want to involve the audience and be an effective storyteller. So this is not the kind of movie that I would sit down by myself and say, 'Eric, I want to write a genre movie about a guy making phone calls and blah, blah, blah.' So you have to become a student and watch movies like this and listen to what a director's trying to achieve, and try and figure out a way to make certain scenes in the movie really effective and legitimately scary and not necessarily campy. I mean there's always going to be campy elements within a movie like this, I think it's inescapable. So without being specific about what I learned, I learned how every movie, every genre creates its own rules of the game. So I had to pay strict attention to what this form demanded and what Jim was looking to achieve to make the best kind of possible movie he could.

"It's always fun to compare yourself to the greats, and I don't mean to, but like Robert Towne has this famous quote because when you're working under other people's work, you're taking shots from across the court that you've never taken before and you're sinking them because you don't care as much. So because this was something I didn't originate and it wasn't my lifeblood in the material, between what Cinetel wanted me to do and what Wynorski wanted me to do, I felt like I could have fun and be creative and if it was a great idea, it was a great idea. If it was a shitty idea, it was a shitty idea and someone will come up with a better idea. At the end of the day, it's really Jim's film more than it is my film so I was just happy to serve and be along for the ride.

"At a certain point later in the process when I became embedded with becoming the re-writer/writer of the script and working closely with Jim and the company, at a certain point someone was banging at my front door, and it was the original writer of the script who was quite incensed when he found out that I was going to be getting kind of like full credit for the screenplay, a screenplay that I hadn't originated. And I kind of just shrugged my shoulders and said, 'I'm really sorry, get the fuck off my porch and call my lawyer because I don't really have anything to do with that.'

"Wynorski has his own ideas in terms of what certain trick genre elements he wants to build into the storytelling. So I sat down elbow to elbow with Jim and did another pass. It probably worked somewhere along those lines. Usually it's a combination of figuring out what the director wants, what the company wants, and figuring out how much freedom I have to get creative. Do I have the ability to switch around these scenes or add new scenes or add new locations? A lot of these movies were really strictly controlled on a budgetary level. And at some point, Brigitte Nielsen became involved so then you figure okay, that might be fun to create this scene or that scene, kind of shape as per making fun of her. I remember there was a fun little scene where, 'you look like Elvira on steroids,' so you try and have a little fun as the talent and the cast becomes more specific in the development of the piece."

Jim Wynorski is no stranger to directing sequels to films he didn't originate. "I always tried to do sequels to movies that weren't so good the first time around. If you're doing a sequel to *The Exorcist*, you're fucked. You're never gonna come up to the original. But if you're doing a sequel to *Big, Bad Mama*, you can do better. If you're doing a sequel to *Deathstalker*, you can do better. If you're doing a sequel to almost anything that wasn't great the first time around, you can try to make it better. It's like when they did a sequel to

Dirty Harry. They hit it with *Magnum Force*, but it wasn't as good as *Dirty Harry*. Even when Lucas did *Empire Strikes Back*, everyone thinks that's the best one, but I still think *Star Wars* is the best one. It's tough to top a great movie and come back with a sequel if it was great to begin with. In all the sequels I was offered, I said fine, let's try it. Let's try and make it better. The first one's always the toughest one to do because you're breaking new ground."

While Patrick O'Bryan's character, Spike, may appear in *976-EVIL II*, it's really the story of Robin Jamison (Debbie James) who is psychically linked with the dean of Slate River College, Professor Stefan Grubeck (René Assa). Grubeck has been killing co-eds with the power he gained via the 976-EVIL "horrorscope" hotline. Spike is Robin's only ally when she tries to stop Professor Grubeck from astral projecting around town to murder witnesses to his crimes, more co-eds, and Robin's buxom friends.

The film cold opens with Laurie Glaser (Karen Mayo-Chandler), a pretty blonde, taking a swim in an empty natatorium. As she swims, the credits play and we get a shot of a phone ringing with a sinister sound as the title appears. Though *976-EVIL 2* been given a subtitle of "The Astral Factor", this seems to be something only shown on the Vestron Video VHS cover (along with the tagline, "This time Satan returns the call").

"The girl in the shower who died is Karen Mayo-Chandler who is now dead for real, and she was dating Jack Nicholson at the time. The girl is there in the beginning strictly to die and run around and be naked, so that was Karen's job." says Wynorski. "She sued the production company because she said she slipped during one of the running sequences and I don't think she ever won the case."

There's no mysterious otherworldly force chasing Laurie. Instead, it's the very corporeal Professor Grubeck who chases her onto the set of Faust which a sign outside the theater proclaims is being directed by Joe Bob Briggs (overseen by Theater Department Head Roger Corman). Grubeck and Laurie are not alone, however, as a hapless janitor, Turrell (George 'Buck' Flower), sees Grubeck impale Laurie with a prop stalactite.

"That was one of the first movies I worked with [George 'Buck' Flower] on," says Wynorski. "He was a great guy and we struck up quite a nice friendship off that show and I think I put him in his last movie which I think, if I'm not mistaken, was *Curse of the Komodo*. I might be wrong but he was in a bunch of my other movies after that. He might have been in *Munchie Strike Back*, I don't know, but that's around when I met him, 1990-1991. Great guy. Hated when he passed. He put me in *Bikini Car Wash Company*, which he produced and Ed Hanson directed. I think they're both gone now. He's what they call 'laugh insurance,' okay? You put Buck Flower in a movie and you're gonna get laughs, especially in the parts I would give him. He was in *Munchie* where he played a drunk, which he was so good at, and I loved working with him."

Spike comes rolling into the film on his motorcycle to a twangy theme by Chuck Cirino. "I first met Chuck in 1969 when a mutual friend introduced us because we had an interest in Ennio Morricone's Spaghetti Western music," says Wynorski. "I became one of his best friends over the years, and when I directed my first movie which was *Lost Empire*, the producers wanted a composer with a little track record, so I had to go with Alan Howarth, but on *Chopping Mall*, I hired Chuck and he's composed a lot of music for me over the years, still does. We're still very good friends. I talk to him all the time. And I asked him to do a kind of Spaghetti Western-esque theme for *976-EVIL II*. And he did. It's a great one, kind of a surf-spaghetti sound. Probably one of the best elements of the movie is the good score by Chuck."

A frequent haunt of Jim Wynorski films, Spike stops off at a strip club for some fries and a beer. We're given a bit of backstory courtesy of a news report on the bar's television where we learn that the Slate River Serial Killer has struck again and that Laurie Glaser was his fifth known victim in four months. Here we're properly introduced to the supernatural element of the film where the bar's stripper (Joy Ballard, who is wearing more clothes than Karen Mayo-Chandler) tells Spike in a demonic voice to "Go back," while a pay phone begins to ring.

"Out of the darkness and into the light comes your horrorscope on this dark and stormy night. Push 666 for your horrorscope now," comes the familiar refrain from *976-EVIL*. "Welcome to the caverns of the unknown, I am the master of the dark, the guide to your destiny on September 15th. Death after death has met your friends, maybe it's time we visited again." When Spike tells the voice to go fuck himself, he's hit with a brilliant beam of holy light which seems to cure him of any future calls.

Spike continues to Slate River where the police have apprehended Professor Grubeck. We're introduced to Sheriff Stone (Paul Coufos) and Deputy Jody Taylor (Philip McKeon), who adds an effective bit of comic relief. It's slightly confusing when Robin Jamison (Debbie James) initially appears in the film as she's another pretty blonde wearing a white top, looking a lot like Laurie did before the stalactite incident.

At the time, Debbie James was dating Paul Hertzberg, making her a shoo-in for the lead of *976-EVIL II*. Jim Wynorski recalls, "This was my first movie with [Paul] so he said, 'You're gonna have your lead.' And that was that. You can't do anything about that. My memory is that she was very beautiful and very cooperative and very vapid. She had little or no personality and it showed in the movie. She was very sweet on the set and was very cooperative. I don't think she had an aptitude for acting. But she sure is pretty."

Robin finds the card for the 976-EVIL hotline amongst some magazines and has a flash to Laurie's death. When she runs into Professor Grubeck and he touches her hand, she gets a full psychic flashback to Laurie's murder. She falls to the floor, only to be revived by her father, Dr. Jamison (Rod McCary).

"I remembered Rod McCary from other pictures and I met him at a restaurant about a week before we cast that role. And I said there's the dad right there," recalls Wynorski.

Professor Grubeck uses his one phone call to ring up 976-EVIL and plead his case for being a faithful servant to the darkness. He's told that he will receive the power he desires, fulfill his purpose, and "feed his fire." There doesn't seem to be any "monkey paw" catch to what Grubeck desires. He revels in being evil and René Assa brings a mirthful mockery to his role. Later in his cell he will gain the power that drives the rest of the film. He can astral project and cause untold mayhem while his body is safely locked away. The only drawback to his newfound ability is that his astral form seems to have a skin condition where he develops more spots as the film goes along.

The first victim of Professor Grubeck's astral form is Turrell, the janitor. Grubeck torments Turrell until he runs into a nearby road where he's splattered like a sack of meat by a semi-truck. After this, Grubeck visits Robin. We've learned that she had something of a crush on him while working for him at Slate River Community College and it seems that he also has feelings for her (this is even more evident by a collection of photos in Grubeck's house).

Of all the diners in all the world, Spike happens upon the one where Robin is having a plate of fries. He finds her again later that night where they have quite a rapport. Spike tells her all about the 976-EVIL number. It isn't until he mentions having visions that she believes him. The two are now fast friends and work to defeat Grubeck's fiendish plans. The film becomes something like a "Scooby-Doo" mystery as Robin and Spike work independently to find clues that might convince Sheriff Stone or Robin's father of the supernatural goings-ons in Slate River.

While Spike searches Grubeck's house he's attacked by appliances and Robin gets zapped by the phone in Grubeck's office, receiving another psychic vision. When she tries to tell her father about it, he dismisses her hysterical raving.

"The effects guys were the biggest doofuses on the planet," recalls Wynorski. "They promised the world and delivered nothing and we had to go outside to get these effects done properly. I think the guy closed his shop the day after the film wrapped. It was like working with dopes. And those shots had to be done over and over and over again. The blue screen was terrible. That was a big fight I had with my producers. I kept saying, 'Take it to my effects guys, take it to my effects guys. They're half as expensive and they're good.' And they wouldn't listen, they'd already hired this guy and he was like the biggest doofus in the world. I don't know where he is today but he's certainly not working in any effects field. He's probably duping other people into spending money they don't have. I don't even remember his name but he was not good."

Unfortunately for Robin, she drives directly into her psychic vision where the prosecutor of Grubeck's case, Susan Lawlor

(Monique Gabrielle), gets a call in her car from Grubeck. Lawlor's vehicle goes completely out of control, smashing into other cars until it crashes into a power station and explodes.

Wynorski recalls, "I was living with Monique Gabrielle at the time, and I remember her coming home one morning after a long night shoot and she just started beating on me because that car chase had made her so sick to her stomach and they were actually hitting her in the car and she came home really bruised. And then I saw the footage and I said, 'Oh this is fantastic footage' and it looks real, like she's being hit by cars and stuff. And then she got even worse mad at me because I had to dub her. She plays the lawyer and they didn't think her voice was authoritative enough so they replaced her voice. It was very disheartening for her."

When Spike and Robin try to figure out how Grubeck could be in his cell and terrorizing motorists, Robin luckily remembers a piece of paper she grabbed from Grubeck's office which mentions "astral research." This leads Spike to Lucifer's, a spooky bookstore (open until Midnight) run by the comely Agnes (Brigette Nielsen).

How did Brigette Nielsen slip into a cameo role in *976-EVIL II*? According to Cat Knell, it was that she had become friends with Brigitte when Knell worked on *Beverly Hills Cop 2*. Knowing that Jim Wynorski's sets were always fun, Knell asked Brigette if she's like to make an appearance. Wynorski remembers it slightly differently, "I was at a Hollywood party and she was there and I was playing pool and she came over and she said, 'Hello,' and I said, 'Hi' and she introduced herself as Brigitte Nielsen and I said, 'Loved you in *Beverly Hills Cop 2*.' And she challenged me to a game of pool. I said 'Let's put some stakes on it. If I lose, I'll put a maid's outfit on, come to your home and clean it. If you lose, you do a day on my film for scale.' And I won."

"She came in and did a day on the film for scale. Very nice lady. She did okay. Patrick O'Bryan was an ass and Brigitte was nice but she didn't know her lines. So, I had to keep doing things over and over and over again. But you never see that when you're watching the movie. You just see the good stuff. You didn't see the outtakes. Plenty of outtakes there."

There's a feeling one gets from most of Jim Wynorski's films of a chaotic glee. His films can mix the deathly serious with slapstick or one-liners, leaving the audience a little off-balance as they never know where the next scene will take them. It's been well-documented just how intense Wynorski's productions can get (see Clay Westervelt's *Popatopolis*) and this manic energy comes through on the screen. It's why things like an appearance from Brigette Nielsen isn't the strangest thing in the movie. It's also why Professor Grubeck appears on a TV screen and zaps Robin's friend Paula (Leslie Ryan) into a mash-up of *It's A Wonderful Life* and *Night of the Living Dead*.

"They were originally playing Pac-Man and somehow the bad guy got the secondary female lead pulled into a Pac-Man game and she was running around being chomped on by those little bubbles and it was a sequence that was gonna cost $65-70 thousand dollars to accomplish and they didn't know what to do with it. They said we don't have the money for this and I said it's all green screen, it's gonna be a financial nightmare," says Wynorski.

"One night I had a nightmare in which I was caught up in *It's a Wonderful Life* and it suddenly turned into *Night of the Living Dead* and I was running from Jimmy Stewart zombies and everything else and I woke up in a sweat. Most people don't remember dreams. This one was so vivid and so cinematically oriented I said the Cinema Angel came down and touched my head and gave me this dream because that usually doesn't happen. And I got up at 5 in the morning, I wrote it down on a piece of paper and I realized I had two public domain movies. I wrote the whole sequence and I must have written it in a morning, it was so vivid. I just wrote what I dreamt and then shot it. And I called Gary Randall, who was my set designer, and I said I want you to go watch both films and then create a set that I can use as both. And we did. And we got some people that looked like the characters and kind of tried to match it all. It was fun to do because we had to use footage from the originals and I didn't have access to the 35mm negative on either of those pictures. So what we had to do was go to the best source at the time which was the laserdisc of *It's Wonderful Life* and transferred it to 35mm film. Then we degraded our image to match that and I don't think we actually used any footage from *Night of the Living Dead*. I just kind of mimicked it. And that's how that sequence came about."

Grubeck frames Robin for Paula's murder. Now on the run, Spike and Robin split up again to pit the astral Grubeck against Spike and the corporeal Grubeck against Robin. This leads to a spectacular stunt sequence as Grubeck goes after Spike in a semi-truck and they kill one another.

"It cost two thousand dollars for the car chase sequence," says Wynorski. "And the car chase took two and a half days and I did not shoot all of it. I shot some of it. Some of it was shot by a guy named Spiro Razatos who I believe gets credit at the end. He's a stuntman and he did a great job with that."

While Spike takes out the astral Professor Grubeck with some dynamite and his motorcycle, Robin runs screaming from the corporeal Grubeck. She leads him to a very tall cliff where Spike can punch him to his death. And, with that, the now-dead Spike disappears into star stuff. Unfortunately, this doesn't convince Robin that anything supernatural has occurred and her sanity (and innocence) get questioned once again—so much so that she's arrested for the wrongful death of Professor Grubeck.

With that, she's thrown into the back of an ambulance and hauled away while a local payphone begins its sinister ring...

Looking like a disheveled Craig Sheffer, *976-EVIL II* marks the end of the brief movie career of Patrick O'Bryan. Jim Wynorski does not remember his experiences with O'Bryan fondly. "Oh my god, I wanted to slap that kid. He was shooting his career in the foot the entire time he was there. Just getting a performance out of him was like pulling teeth. Kind of a nice guy off the set, but oh my god, we'd butt heads so many times on that picture. And he played like The Fonz and I didn't know what he was doing. I think they had to have him to tie it into the first one. But it saddled me with an actor that was just an annoyance. Please feel free to print that, too. I cut him out as much as I could. I did everything I could to say, 'Go back to your trailer, Pat, and enjoy your TV show.' And as you see, I never worked with him again. Why would I subject myself to that kind of stuff? You get enough trouble while making a movie. He was destined for flipping burgers and I don't know what he's doing now. He might be the head of a studio for all I know, but I just thought he was very uncooperative. The thing is Pat had some acting ability but he was just an annoyance, he thought he was Steve McQueen. A total pain in the fucking ass."

One Easter Egg, or rather, Easter Rabbit that people should watch for in *976-EVIL II*: "In every sequence, there's a rabbit. Not in every shot, but in every sequence, there's a rabbit. It's like, find the rabbit in every sequence. For no good reason, I tried to put a rabbit into every sequence. Sometimes it's wallpaper, sometimes it's bed sheets, sometimes it's a live rabbit, sometimes it's a ceramic rabbit. There's a rabbit in every sequence. I announced that at the screening when they had a screening of the movie before the film came out. I announced that and everybody was just shouting 'rabbit, rabbit.' And I hadn't told anyone, including the producers that, and none of the producers who had seen the movie six times, ever noticed that there was a rabbit in every sequence. Some of them are tough to find on video, but they're there. And if you look hard enough, you see them."

INNER SANCTUM
by Mark Thomas McGee

B-Movie Makes A-Movie Money. That was the headline on *The Wall Street Journal* more than a quarter of a century ago. The B-movie in question was a two-bit, direct-to-video crime drama called *Inner Sanctum* which had, to everyone's surprise, grossed over six million record-breaking dollars, making its director a minor celebrity among the filmmakers on Hollywood's new Poverty Row. As the writer of the film I was walking on air. I wrote a hit movie and even though my contribution had little to do with its success the title would look good on my resume.

It took me a month to write *Inner Sanctum*. That's a decent amount of time. I've had as little as two days. I was proud of that script. It had some twists and turns and it all made sense. That must sound delusional to anyone who has seen the film but it's true. Understand, I'm not saying it was a good script. How can a writer be objective about his own work? But it made sense. So what happened? The short answer: Tanya Roberts. If you want the long answer, read on.

First, a little background on *Inner Sanctum*. For ten years it was a popular radio program that spun tales of mystery with a little supernatural seasoning. A few years after the show's premier in 1941, Universal Studios produced six low budget Inner Sanctum mysteries with their resident horror star, Lon Chaney Jr. They were cheaply made, routine programmers. Nothing to get excited about unless you're Fred Ray and you happen to be a big fan of Lon Chaney and low end movies.

Fred had probably made fifteen or twenty pictures when I met him. He's probably made a hundred more since but he's convinced that the only one he'll be remembered for is *Hollywood Chainsaw Hookers*. Fred probably couldn't name a single film in William Wyler's canon but he could rattle of a list of Al Adamson's movies without a second's thought. When he told me he wanted to make *Inner Sanctum* it didn't seem to me that he could have set the bar any lower.

In his autobiography, *In the Arena*, Charlton Heston boldly critiqued his own performance in each of the films in his fantastic body of work and was pleased to discover, when all was said and done, that he was the greatest actor who ever lived. Heston wrote that shortly before production began on *The Omega Man*, which was based on the novel *I Am Legend* by Richard Matheson, he and some of the big wigs filed into a little screening room to watch *The Last Man on Earth*, a movie starring Vincent Price that was based on the same novel. When it was over and the lights came on, Heston arrogantly remarked: "We can do better than that."

And that's how I felt when Fred told me he wanted to make *Inner Sanctum*. I figured we couldn't do any worse. Well, Charlton Heston was wrong and so was I. *The Omega Man* made *The Last Man on Earth* look like a work of genius. Our *Inner Sanctum* made those old Chaney movies seem like milestones in cinema art. It just shows what you can do when you put your mind to something.

Initially, Fred was going to make *Inner Sanctum* with his own money, which meant there'd be just enough in the budget to run film through the camera. He would shoot the whole thing in an old two story frame house in Los Angeles someplace and by the whole thing I mean exactly that. The entire story would have played out in the confines of the house, much like a stage play. The camera would have hopped from room to room, maybe even getting as far as the backyard, but it would have never be bold enough to breech the property line. Claustrophobic filmmaking at its finest. But when we sat down to work out the details of the script, Fred and I were working with a bigger budget. Not huge, mind you, only $650,000, but it was enough to get us out of the damn house. Fred must have sold the project at that point.

More than anything, I wanted access to the house next door. Anyone making a thriller can get a lot of mileage out of a house next door. The burning glow of a cigarette in a darkened room late at night. The glare of the sun off of a pair of binoculars. The silhouette of someone watching from behind a curtain in an upstairs window. Mystery. Suspense. Excitement. You can get all of these things from the house next door. But I had no idea what it would cost and I knew that any amount of money on a low budget movie is a major expense. You really have to make every penny count and I didn't know if Fred would think it was worth it. Fortunately, he did. We didn't even dicker about it. Fred is a reasonable guy.

So we had the house, the house next door, an office and a reception area. Now we could tell our story. It was that old wheeze about the husband who wants to kill his wife for her money. What the heck, it was good enough for Alfred Hitchcock. Only this time around (and this was Fred's idea and a good one, too) we would muddy the water so much that the audience would never quite be sure of who was doing what to who for most of the picture. Unfortunately, the way things worked out, the audience never did find out.

Our goal from the beginning was to deceive the audience without playing them for suckers. No cheats. Just the other night I watched this very smart movie about four magicians who pull off these massive robberies. The cop on their trail is obsessed with their capture. Surprise! The cop turns out to be the mastermind. Yet everything the cop said and did throughout the picture told a different story. Everything! People who make these kinds of movies hope the audience will either forget the details or assume they misinterpreted a lot of stuff. I couldn't have been more than five or six when I saw some murder mystery with a ghost in it, some woman in one of those white, flowing gowns, transparently roaming the house. Toward the end of the movie the hero dramatically reached into a closet and pulled out a sheet on a wire. "Here's your ghost!" he announced triumphantly. There was no misinterpreting that. Fred and I didn't want to pull those kind of shenanigans.

At first I was annoyed at having to follow the *Inner Sanctum* formula of letting the audience hear what the protagonist is thinking from time to time. It was too melodramatic for my taste, but it was something that Fred insisted on and it proved to be a useful tool because our protagonist, Jennifer Reed, was not very likeable. She's self-centered, slightly paranoid, and gutless. The first time we see her she's trying to commit suicide and she makes a mess of that. Ends up in a wheelchair. Only when the audience hears what she's thinking, how frightened she is and how helpless she feels, does she earn any sympathy.

Throughout her marriage Jennifer has falsely accused her husband Baxter of infidelity. At the moment she believes he's having an affair with Anna Rollins, one of the trainees at the insurance company where Baxter works. "When the hell would I have time?" he asks her. "When I'm not at work I'm taking care of you." After he leaves we hear what she's thinking. "Every day I push Bax further away from me. Sometimes I wonder if I deliberately fell. Maybe I wanted to cripple myself so he'd stay...out of pity. Am I going mad?"

For once she's right about Baxter. He'd love to have an affair with Anna Rollins. So would his other trainee, Jeff Siegel. Anna likes Jeff but she's in love with Baxter. She does her best to keep him at arm's length because she doesn't want to get involved with a married man.

Trapped in a loveless marriage, Baxter has all but accepted his unhappy lot in life when Jennifer's doctor drops the big bomb. Jennifer's paralysis is in all in her mind. Baxter feels betrayed. Worse, he feels like a dope. And he starts to thinking that maybe, just maybe, there might be a way to spring the trap.

Against Jennifer's wishes Baxter hires a full-time nurse. And what a nurse! Young. Pretty. Her name is Lynn Foster. Jennifer takes an immediate disliking to her. She tries to injure herself in the hope of getting Lynn fired. Her plan backfires and she ends up taking a spill. Baxter starts to rake her over the coals but Lynn takes the blame. She tells Baxter that she was the one who forgot to set the brake on Jennifer's wheelchair. Jennifer is grateful and lets her guard down a little with Lynn after that.

It doesn't take Lynn but a few minutes to size up the situation at the Reed house. "You don't care much for your wife, do you, Mr. Reed?" she observes. "That's all I've been doing, lady," he replies. "Now it's your turn."

Besides being young and pretty, Lynn Foster is also the subject of an on-going police investigation. The cops think she may have murdered a woman in her care, then turned around and married the woman's husband and murdered him too. (I stole that idea from *Double Indemnity*.) Both of her victims were insured with Baxter's company. Baxter came across Lynn's file quite by accident when he was looking for a file in the claims department. It started him thinking. Who better to take the fall for Jennifer's murder than a suspect in a double homicide?

If Baxter had worked in claims he would have known that his company had hired a private investigator named Neil Semple to keep tabs on Lynn. And what better way to do it than to move into… the house next door. Jennifer sees him at the window with his camera and his binoculars and assumes that he's spying on her, being the paranoid mess that she is. And when she sees Baxter talking to the guy late one night she wonders if they might be in cahoots in some plot to... To what? She doesn't know exactly but it all looks very suspicious. She shares her fears with Lynn who thinks the new neighbor is probably a peeping Tom. She doesn't tell Jennifer that she knows all about Neil Semple. And when she's had time to put two and two together, she knows what Baxter has up his sleeve, too.

Anna Rollins shows up one morning at the Reed residence with the exciting news that she sold a group insurance plan to a big chain. When she sees Lynn she's certain she's seen her before. And then she remembers, the face in a photograph that fell out of one of the files in Baxter's office. Anna enlists the aid of Jeff Siegel to help her search for it. They're interrupted by Baxter who is anything but pleased to see them ransacking his office. On the way out, Jeff spots the file they've been looking for in Baxter's trash. After everyone has gone home for the night, Jeff returns to Baxter's office, plucks the file out of the trash and phones Anna to give her the lowdown on Lynn Foster, alias Lynn Comstock. Jeff is about to hang up when Baxter shoves a knife into his ribs and throws him through the window. Siegel falls to his death, courtesy of a clip from one of Fred's other movies. If Fred hadn't had the shot, Jeff Siegel would have died in some less dramatic way.

The next morning Lynn accuses Baxter of hiring Neil Semple to kill Jennifer. She knows better but she has a plan. By the time their conversation is over she has convinced Baxter that Jennifer had been the one to hire Semple. To kill him. Baxter refuses to believe it until Lynn breaks the news that Jennifer now knows that she didn't fall down the stairs. She knows that Baxter pushed her.

At the very beginning of the story Jennifer is shown awake in bed, staring at Baxter. "Who are you dreaming about, Bax?" she wonders. "I know it isn't me. Jesus, I can't go on like this." She crawls out of bed, goes downstairs and swallows a bunch of sleeping pills. At first she's angry that it's taking so long, then gets scared when they start to take effect and realizes that she doesn't want to die after all. She calls to Baxter but her voice is too weak. It takes all of her strength to climb the stairs. Her legs have turned to mush. "Keep moving," she tells herself. "You must keep moving!" Finally, after what seems like a million years, she clears the last step, passes out and takes a hard roll down the stairs. But in that moment before she lost consciousness she saw Baxter's angry face just before he pushed her. She'd done her best to suppress that memory but it had been eating into her nightmares and she couldn't hold it at bay any longer.

At the office the next morning Anna is trying to come to grips with the fact that she might be in love with a murderer. She asks Baxter point blank if he killed Jeff Siegel and if he hired Lynn to kill his wife. Baxter admits to wanting to kill his wife but he blames Jeff's murder on Lynn because he doesn't want Anna to hate him. But he does want her to forget about him. But it's too late. Anna is hopelessly in love with him and after listening to all of the reasons she shouldn't be, she cries: "I don't care. I don't care. I don't care." So he has to tell her the truth about Jeff Siegel. It's Baxter's moment. His one good deed. And as we all know, no good deed goes unpunished, especially in film noir.

Believing that Neil Semple is out to get him, Baxter allows Lynn to orchestrate a showdown that ends when Baxter pumps Semple full of lead. Lynn photographs the event and threatens to send the photographs to the police if Baxter doesn't cut her in on the money he'll inherit when *they* kill Jennifer. Clearly, Lynn is the one in charge at this point and now that there is no one to take the rap for Jennifer's murder, they agree to forget about the insurance money. Either they'll drive Jennifer to suicide or make her death look like a suicide.

Fearing for Jennifer's life, Anna phones her and tells her to get out of the house. Her life is in danger. Anna has already phoned the police. They're on the way. And so is she. In fact, Anna arrives ahead of the police, in time to stop Baxter and Lynn from drowning Jennifer in the family pond. Anna smacks Baxter in the side of the head with a shovel. But before she can give Lynn more of the same, Lynn takes the shovel away from her and jabs the handle into her belly. With Anna doubled over Lynn turns her attention back to Jennifer who is spitting up water, still trying to catch her breath. Lynn forces Jennifer's head back into the pond and it looks like curtains for Jennifer when miracle of miracles she finds the strength in her legs to push Lynn away. With her paralysis melting away, Jennifer stands on her own two feet and delivers a hard left to Lynn's jaw. Lynn falls on her back. Jennifer straddles her and beats the crap out of her. Anna has to pull her off. In the distance we hear police sirens. In the nick of time. As usual.

Okay. The script is done. I'm happy with it. And Fred and I are on our way to Universal to meet with Mark Damon. Damon used to be an actor. He was in *The Party Crashers* and *House of Usher*. Things like that. Now he was a producer. *Das Boot. Short Circuit.* Things like that. He was the executive producer on our show. A fellow named Alan Amiel was the producer. Alan had worked with Fred before on *Deep Space*.

Damon didn't have much to say about the script. The only changes he wanted was the addition of three sex sequences. Because Tanya Roberts was going to be in picture.

Tanya Roberts was the gorgeous actress who replaced Shelly Hack on the 5th (and last) season of *Charlie's Angeles*. She was Zelda in the TV pilot for Mike Hammer with Stacey Keach but she opted out of the series to star in *Sheena, Queen of the Jungle*, one of the biggest duds of the year. And she had just made a direct-to-video movie called *Night Eyes*, a steamy little thriller that was anything but a dud, box-office-wise that is. It was Tanya's softcore sex scenes that made the film a hit. Mark Damon wanted to cash in while Tanya was still hot.

It would have been nice if our witty dialog and clever plotting had sold the script but obviously that was not the case. Damon probably didn't give our script anymore thought than he would have given the cab that took him to the airport. It was simply something he needed.

Looking out of the large picture window in Damon's office, Fred and I were startled by a sudden burst of flame as a fire broke out in the studio. Then, without any provocation that I recall, Mark Damon made a remarkable statement. He claimed that he directed *The Pit and the Pendulum* which we both knew had been directed by Roger Corman. According to Damon, he and Corman made a deal. If Damon would agree to be in *House of Usher* Corman would let him direct *The Pit and the Pendulum*. Damon has repeated this fantasy a number of times since but this was the first time that either one of us had heard it and we were caught with our mouths open. We wondered why a guy who was doing very well for himself would need to take credit for some obscure Vincent Price B-movie. I wanted to tell him that I directed *Lawrence of Arabia*. But Mark Damon held my paycheck. So I held my tongue.

Anyway, the sex scenes were added with little trouble and my job was done. Or so I thought. But a problem arose when Tanya decided that she didn't want to play a villain. The easy fix would have been to have her switch roles but Anna Rollins was a supporting part and nobody involved in the project wanted to see Tanya in a wheelchair, so that really wasn't an option. Alan Amiel always wanted Tanya to play the nurse. He wrongly believed it was the nurse's movie. He and Fred got into a disagreement about it. I was as green as any kid from a pea patch but I knew Tanya would get her way. After all, she *was* the movie.

Not everyone realizes (or cares and why should they?) that constructing a script is like building a house of cards. Remove one card and the whole thing falls apart. Knowing that, Alan Amiel wanted to preserve as much of the script as he could and still keep the boss happy. What he was trying to avoid was a major rewrite. The clock was ticking. There wasn't time for a major rewrite. Alan and company wanted to get the show on the road.

Producers will often bring in another writer at a lower rate to fix a script but Alan and company didn't want to take the time to bring another writer up to speed and I knew the thing inside and out. Like I said, they were in a hurry. So I went with Alan to Tanya's lovely home in the hills to discuss the changes she wanted to make. I thought Fred should have been the one to go but he was happy to let me go in his stead. Mighty happy. The son of the bitch knew something that I didn't.

Barry Roberts ushered Alan and I into the house. He was Tanya's husband. They'd met while waiting in line to see a movie and got married a few weeks later. Barry wrote a script for Tanya to star in. *Legal Tender*. To my knowledge it remains his only credit.

Barry told us to make ourselves at home. I sat on the nearest sofa and Barry plopped down beside me and made a vulgar remark about his wife. He said it with the authority of a man who knows of what he speaks, and while I don't doubt for a second the validity of his remark, the jerk should have kept it to himself.

Tanya finally showed up, looking like a million bucks. Besides having a fantastic body, her eyes are incredible. Hypnotic. Someone told me she uses something called Eye Bleach. I never heard of it. Anyway, after the obligatory introductions, Tanya pulled me to one side and said, as though she were confiding in me, "I hope they don't want me to do any sex scenes because I'm not doing any more of those."

All right you people, listen up. We're going to remake King Kong *but this time without the damn monkey.*

I thought she was kidding. She looked sincere but after all she's an actress. I have to admit I was confused. Hadn't she read the script? The scenes were there. It wasn't something they were going to spring on her at the last minute. In retrospect I came to the conclusion that she may have been laying the foundation for a salary hike. But why tell me? I'm only the writer. I say *only* because that's the way writers are thought of by everyone in Hollywood but Darryl Zanuck and he's dead. Writers aren't second class citizens. They're illegal aliens. I was once invited to the set of some piece of junk I had written to watch a bunch of women cavorting around in the altogether. It is common practice to clear the set of everyone but essential personnel whenever you're shooting nudity but the room I was in was packed with window shoppers, their eyes glued to the young lady in the shower, acting as if the spray of the water was some sort of an aphrodisiac. She was running her hands across her more than ample breasts when she suddenly froze and locked eyes with the director. "Why are there so many people here?" she asked peevishly. "You can't tell me of these people need to be here. Jesus Christ! Even the writer is here!"

Even the writer. I felt like I was three feet tall. And just to be sure I understood my place, I was asked to leave.

I was the only one.

Anyway, we're at Tanya's house. She's sitting on one side of the room and Alan is sitting on the other. Both of them have scripts in their laps and are running their fingers slavishly over each and every line. Barry is pacing back and forth, throwing his two cents in now and then.

Alan keeps saying, "So, it is okay up to this point," and Tanya says that it is and on they plod. I could have shown them the page they were looking for but Tanya had to be the one to find it. I couldn't very well take the nap I wanted so I let my mind wander instead.

All at once I found myself in the middle of a shit storm. Tanya and Barry were on their feet, in the middle of the room, screaming at each other. Good Golly, Miss Molly! I had never seen two people carry on so. The level of rage was astronomical. They were shouting loud enough to be heard in Arizona. And I'm sitting there thinking: People, we're talking about *Inner Sanctum*. How serious can it be?

Once Tanya and Barry had exhausted themselves and the room was quiet again, the four of us carried on as if nothing had happened. It was rather like being in the Twilight Zone. But it proved to be the calm before the storm. Before long they were at it again, and so it went for the rest of the afternoon. It was clear to me now why Fred had chosen to sit this one out. He'd seen this show before.

I always brought a tape recorder with me to script meetings because I was often guilty of hearing what I wanted to hear. I've walked away thinking I knew exactly what the producers wanted only to find, after playing the tape, that I had my head up my ass. The tape always set me straight. By the same token, producers will often say things that they will later deny having said. The machine sets them straight too. The tape I made of Tanya and Barry that afternoon was quite a hit with my friends. They couldn't believe it. I later saw a video that someone had secretly shot of Tanya and Barry going through their antics on the set of one of her movies. Robert Downey looked like he was in a state of shock. Just as she'd start to settle down, Barry would say something to fire her up again. Someone finally put their hand over Barry's mouth. It will probably come as no surprise that Barry was not allowed on the set of *Inner Sanctum*.

A friend once told me he would gladly give his scripts away for free if the producers would pay for the meetings. If I had been paid a million dollars for that meeting with Tanya and Barry it wouldn't have been enough. It would have helped but it wouldn't have been enough.

Alas, Alan's best efforts to save the script, while valiant, were doomed from the start. The script needed major surgery and I'm sorry to report that it never fully recovered because Tanya didn't know the difference between motivation and what she called a back story. Here is one example. In the revised version, Lynn is still a suspect in a pair of murders but she's innocent. Neil Semple, the P.I. on her tail, has fallen in love with her and believes that she's innocent. In an effort to clear her name, the two conspire to bring Baxter Reed to justice.

"That's back story," Tanya insisted. "The audience doesn't need to know that."

And so the audience is left to wonder why the private eye helping Tanya instead of spying on her like he's supposed to do. And what are they up to? No reason for you to know, according to Tanya. I told her that somewhere along the line we'd have to pay for all of this secrecy. It became clear that I would have to write a tag sequence, like at the end of *Psycho*, where someone ties up all the loose ends. They did it every week on *Perry Mason*. Of course you run the risk of boring your audience to death. They've seen the end of the story. They wanna go home. So I wrote, rewrote, and wrote the tag sequence again until I couldn't write it any shorter. It was six pages.

"Cut it to three," Mark Damon told me.

So I did. I wasn't able to tie up as many of the loose ends, but I got the big chunks.

I don't visit sets very often. No matter where I stand I'm in the way. Besides, making movies is boring. Everything takes sooooo long. But if you want to write movies you need to see how they're made. You need to understand how it all comes together so that you don't write something they can't afford to shoot. You'll learn a lot of valuable stuff. One thing I learned: The performance you see in front of you is *not* the one you see on film. Anthony Hopkins told a story about the time one of his friends landed a part in a Robert Mitchum movie. Hopkins was envious. Mitchum was one of his favorites and he'd always wanted to watch him work. "You didn't miss a thing," his friend told him after the first day. "Mitchum was terrible. He was just walking through it." The next day his friend called again. "Forget what I said. I just saw the rushes. Mitchum was running rings around all of us." In reverse, I thought Valerie Waldman was giving a fabulous performance as Jennifer until I saw the rushes. She was a little too much. I need to add that overall I thought she gave a good account of herself in a difficult part. She told me she was really happy to get it and that every actress in town wanted it.

Really?!

Alan was in a snit the day I came to the set. I saw him across the room engaged in a conversation with someone and he looked upset. Then, horror of horrors, he saw me and started coming my way. Had I been near an exit I would have made a run for it. "You've got to help me," he said. "Tanya is rewriting her dialog and she can't write." He gave me her revised dialog and told me to fix it. I knew it was pointless but I gave Alan what he asked for and then beat a hasty retreat before he could return with her rewrite of my rewrite.

Whatever Tanya wants, Tanya gets.

I don't remember how long the film had been in production when the front office asked for an additional sequence. They wanted to get out of the house again and thought another sequence at the insurance company was the cheapest possible way to do it. Specifically, they wanted a pair of cops to grill Baxter about Jeff Siegel's murder. It was a sequence designed to be an island unto itself. Whatever happened, it couldn't affect anything that followed it. In other words, you could cut it and no one would know the difference.

In my opinion the sequence that should have been added was the visit to the doctor's office when Baxter learns that Jennifer's paralysis is all in her mind. As written Baxter and Jennifer are shown returning home from the doctor and we slowly learn the reason he looks so angry. Dramatically speaking, it would have been much better to see their faces when the doctor broke the news. The conversation that followed could have been pretty lively too. It was a missed opportunity.

Fred shot some inserts with Michelle Bauer that day. Michelle is a lovely lady who'd made several movies with Fred, including *Hollywood Chainsaw Hookers*. Michelle was serving as a body double for Margaux Hemmingway, the actress playing Anna Rollins. Although Margaux took the part knowing she would have to do nudity she wasn't happy about it. Unlike Tanya, she was pretty stingy with her nakedness. In the middle of a heated grab fest with actor Joseph Bottoms (our Baxter Reed), she pushed him away with disgust before the scene was over, and with her tit hanging out of her blouse she said, "That's enough!" She was thoroughly disgusted. Unlike Margaux, Michelle wasn't shy about showing her body. "I don't think anybody's going to want to see it," I heard her say. "Everybody's seen my saggy tits."

Frankly, it's too bad Michelle Bauer wasn't the star of the movie. Everyone concerned would have been better off. Michelle wouldn't have thrown tantrums or hissy fits, she would have stayed sober, and she wouldn't have been a monkey in the wrench. Tanya's narcissistic and disruptive behavior during the making of this picture was happily documented by that bastion of fearless truth-seeking, *The Enquirer.* "Every word was true," Fred told me.

Of course there was screening of the movie for the cast and crew and of course I attended. I was more interested in how my dialog sounded than anything else. You don't know it works until you hear it. Of course the actor has to be good enough to sell it. Anyway, that was my main concern. I didn't have much hope for the movie. Good thing, too.

First we see an establishing shot of the house at night. Inside Jennifer and Baxter's bedroom the lights are off and he's in bed asleep. She's awake. And the room is so bright you could read a book. And everything that followed was too bright. No mood. No nothing. We were definitely starting out on the wrong foot.

The first exchange between Baxter and Jennifer was equally disheartening. Baxter wasn't supposed to be mean. He was supposed to be tired. Fed up. Joseph Bottoms turned him into an angry, sleazy turd. Maybe that's what Fred wanted. I never asked and there was nothing to be done about it now. But it was a one-note, Snidley Whiplash performance and not a very good one at that.

And then there was Miss Hemmingway. Honestly, if I had known she was going to have so much trouble pronouncing the name Bax I would have changed it to Bob. She comes close to sabotaging just about every scene she's in.

Now we come to the scene were the audience learns that someone is spying on Jennifer and Lynn. I thought of a cool way to impart this important piece of information. The camera is just outside of the window. We hear Jennifer and Lynn talking inside. The camera moves away from the house until we can't hear them anymore. Then, as the camera moves closer to the house next door we hear them again, only this time through a speaker. I guess Fred didn't think it was so cool. He changed it. We see Jennifer's house through the window of the house next door and hear their voices from the speaker near the window. It's not as interesting or dramatic but it works. Except there was a gap in the conversation as I wrote it and now the gap wasn't needed. So someone needed to write something that married the last line before the gap to the first line after it. But nobody did. The scary part is nobody noticed it didn't make sense. They didn't notice or they didn't care. It doesn't speak well for anyone involved no matter which way you look at it.

I'd rather not dwell on the sex sequences except to say that they bring the film to a grinding halt. Let's move on to the big finish. Jennifer saves Lynn, they stagger back into the house with their arms around each other, the film fades and...it's over! There was no tag sequence. I was stunned. I didn't know they hadn't filmed it. And I never found out why they didn't.

Whenever I asked a friend of mine what he thought of some movie that he wrote he would always say: "It has moments." That's how I feel about *Inner Sanctum*. It has moments. Not enough to make it a good movie but that's the way it goes. Chuck Cirino's score was okay. Valerie Waldman is good enough. And I liked Tanya Roberts. I thought she was fun. Should you ever see the film please note that she wears a new outfit in every sequence. She insisted on it. And then took it all with her, bless her heart. $50,000 and a new wardrobe. Not bad for a couple of weeks work.

No one could have been more surprised than I was when our humble little messed up movie became a hit. It not only defied logic, it defied McGee's law which says that once something starts trouble it's always trouble. *Inner Sanctum* should have tanked. I couldn't understand why it didn't. I didn't realize the story wasn't over yet. I didn't know I'd be asked to write more erotic thrillers. For Tanya Roberts! That's when McGee's law went into overdrive. But that, my friend, is a story for another time.

Breakdown

by Mike Malloy

The indie-movie boom of the 1990s (think *Pulp Fiction*, *Chasing Amy*, and *Boogie Nights*) offered easily accessible alternatives for mainstream audiences looking to escape exploding helicopters and star-driven fluff. As poorly as some of these '90s independents have aged, they seemed fresh and original at the time, and the boom drew comparisons to the way a tired Tinseltown received a makeover in the early '70s with the "New Hollywood" movement.

This is not to say '90s audiences didn't plunk down admission money for the helicopters and the fluff. They did so in droves, in fact, giving the decade a scad of movies like *Jurassic Park*, *Independence Day* and the *Batman* sequels. So noisy franchise films held their own, even in the decade's zeitgeist of small independent films focused on story and style.

In 1997, along came Jonathan Mostow's *Breakdown*, a film which straddled the divide. *Breakdown* was, in some ways, a throwback to the small-cast, fish-out-of-water "everyman" stories that the '70s favored (*Deliverance, Duel*, etcetera). It would, in fact, end up being reviewed by *Entertainment Weekly*'s Lisa Schwarzbaum as, "so casual, so comfortable with its own small expectations ([including] a good but unglamorous cast, a sturdy but unspectacular plot)." Hardly typical summer blockbuster material.

But in its conclusion, Mostow's film is a stunts-oriented slam-banger, complete with a car chase involving a tractor-trailer, fiery explosions, a precipitous canyon bridge and lots of death defying (and even a little death itself).

The film's actual content wasn't the only way *Breakdown* straddled the studio-versus-independent divide; the way the film was produced was also a weird amalgam. Mostow's film received rejections from all major studios for a front-end pickup. It somehow proceeded independently as a big-budgeted film nonetheless. And before it could be completed, it was under the Paramount Pictures banner in time for its release.

Breakdown began life, according to writer-director Jonathan Mostow, as a screenplay idea born out of another, unproduced film project.

"We'd actually gotten to the point of even going and scouting locations," explains Mostow, during a 2011 interview, about the earlier project that fizzled. "And it was a movie that took place in the desert, and it involved some trucks. And so I just had in my mind these locations and the imagery of some of these 18-wheeler trucks in my head. And just one day . . . I just thought, 'What's another story I could do in the desert with trucks?' It's kind of a crazy way to come about thinking of a movie. But this idea just popped into my head. And I said to myself, 'Gee, that's a story that compels me.' And I wrote it very quickly. I wrote the script in three weeks."

At the time, Mostow had been working closely with legendary Italian-born producer Dino De Laurentiis, who then had offices in Los Angeles.

"I came to know Dino about six years before I made *Break-down*," recalls Mostow. "And my contact with Dino came because I was making a very low-budget . . . a movie at the time called *Flight of Black Angel*. And it was a very ambitious film in that we were making it for less than a million dollars but it was a jet-fighter action thriller. And we not surprisingly found ourselves going a little over budget, and the people putting up the money had run out of money and were basically saying, 'Look, you've just got to finish the movie the way that it is.'"

But Mostow wanted proper finishing funds for the film. The writer-director says a way out of this dilemma appeared at his weekly poker game, when one of the other players—a business associate of De Laurentiis—invited him to the longtime producer's offices to screen a portion of *Black Angel*. The poker buddy conceded that it was a "crazy idea."

"A couple days later, I went to Dino's offices with a couple reels of the film and projected it in his theater with him sitting a couple rows in front of me. At the end, the lights came up, and he turned to my friend and said, 'Okay, give him the money.' And at the end of the day, I had a check to finish the movie, and in exchange Dino got the rights to some foreign territories—a couple countries. He wound up doing very well with that. So he became interested in doing another movie with me."

Mostow says that after that first experience, he developed some other projects with De Laurentiis that didn't get produced. And the 2004 biography *Dino: The Life and Films of Dino De Laurentiis* notes that Mostow was the producer's pick to direct the 1996 Ray Liotta-starring thriller *Unforgettable*—a pick that was vetoed by MGM Pictures President Michael Marcus.

Mostow had written *Breakdown* on spec, but says that he had a "first look" deal with De Laurentiis. Mostow's mentor exercised his prerogative, and according to the *Dino* biography, the famous producer loved the story because it was a work of fiction that could very easily be true.

The story involves a middle-class, middle-aged couple—Jeff (Kurt Russell) and Amy (Kathleen Quinlan)—traveling from Boston to San Diego as they relocate for new work. Deciding to take the scenic route in their new Jeep Cherokee, they're driving in a desolate stretch of the Southwest when their truck stalls out, leaving them stranded on the side of the road in the middle of nowhere. A trucker (J.T. Walsh) soon passes by and agrees to give Amy a ride to a diner, where she can phone for help (his C.B. radio is conveniently kaput). Help never arrives, and when Jeff eventually makes it to the diner, there's no sign of Amy. The everyman husband then launches into a heroic crusade to find his wife in this strange land, and he uncovers a plot involving abductions, blackmail and murder.

"When you are traveling far from home, there's a certain paranoia, a certain anxiety that kicks in," says Mostow of the film's universally relatable quality. "It's true when we were cavemen and we were far from our own caves. You're away from the security of home."

Mostow says the story is also relatable to everyone who's ever had their imaginations spurred by traveling through desolate areas, far away from civilization.

"You see somebody living in a little house or trailer out in the middle of nowhere, half a mile off the main road. And you think to yourself, 'Who lives there? What's going on there?' . . . And if you have any paranoid thoughts, your mind starts to spin out different scenarios."

With this story involving a small cast and more tension than stunts, *Breakdown* had the potential to be made very cheaply.

"Initially, we were going to make it very low-budget . . . $4 million, all in," says Mostow. "[Dino] said, 'Who do you want?' And I said, 'I wrote it with Kurt Russell in mind.' So he made an offer to Kurt."

According to a May 4, 1997 *Virginian-Pilot* newspaper interview, Russell said he liked De Laurentiis and he liked the script.

But there was a problem.

"Kurt's a very devoted father," says Mostow. "He had an arrangement with Goldie [Hawn, his longtime domestic partner] that neither one would ever do two films in a row. They always scheduled to film to switch off, so that there would always be a parent at home. They would never go off and simultaneously do films."

Mostow says that Hawn had already booked a movie, one that he remembers as being shot in Paris (this was likely Woody Allen's *Everyone Says I Love You*). The Paris film was a movie to be made on

Hawn's turn, as Russell would have just finished John Carpeneter's *Escape from L.A.* by then. But Mostow and Dino took a meeting with Russell and his agent nonetheless.

"[Kurt] said, 'I have to be home in the evening when my kids get home,'" says Mostow. "Dino said, 'No problem.' I looked at Dino. What do you mean, 'No problem?' We're shooting this movie 1500 miles away. How's that no problem? So what we did was: His deal had what was called a 'twelve-hour turnaround' from his doorstep in Pacific Palisades. So it meant that if we picked him up at seven in the morning, he had to be back at his house at seven in the evening."

According to the *Virginian-Pilot* interview, Russell also had a stipulation that he had to be wrapped by the end of the school year. The deal was made, and Russell, who was commanding $10 million per picture at the time, was reportedly paid up to $15 million for *Breakdown*.

"Dino had guaranteed Kurt's salary, so even if there was no movie to get made at that point, Dino was already in hot water," says Mostow.

Russell was at the height of his leading-man stardom at the time, having just been in action hits like *Executive Decision*, *Stargate* and *Tombstone*. But no U.S. studio wanted to make the film, even with the bankable Russell attached, and even with some funding already in place.

"We had sixty percent of the financing coming from a foreign source," says Mostow. "Aaron Spelling had a company that sold rights to movies internationally. So Aaron Spelling's company was putting up sixty percent of the movie. So we really just needed less than half the financing from a U.S. studio, and no studio wanted to put up the money. One studio even said, 'If you replace the director, we'd do it. But this guy's only done one little movie, and we want to put a big-name director on it.' And Dino, to his credit, said, 'Nope. I change studios, but I don't change directors.' He then proceeded to basically risk his own money, and we started shooting the movie with no U.S. studio distribution deal in place, which is unheard of in Hollywood."

Also, despite the attachment of high-profile star Russell, the production had a difficult time finding a leading lady.

"We'd been getting passed on," says Mostow. "We'd sent it to some actresses, and they'd said 'no,' because they'd read the script and realize they disappear on page ten, and basically they're out of the movie [until the climax]. Who wants to play that?"

Considering the minimal on-screen time of the part, getting an actress that was then currently nominated for an Oscar might seem *even more* difficult than other actresses. But in fact, the nomination was the very reason Mostow landed the casting of Kathleen Quinlan—then nominated for an Academy Award (for *Apollo 13*) and in the throes of Oscar week. The director says Quinlan's agent set up a meeting, despite the fact that the actress was slammed with all her obligations regarding the Oscar ceremony forthcoming in a few days.

"She was super, super busy. But we were about to start shooting, because we were running out of time. And so we prevailed upon her. She lived in Malibu. [Her representatives] said, 'If you can go out to Malibu and meet her at the Starbucks near her house, she'll meet you for 15 minutes.' So I went out to Malibu, and what I discovered was that she had not read the script."

"It gave me a chance to pitch to her not only the story in a way that would intrigue her, but also why—even though she was off-screen—she was a critical component of the movie. And what I explained to her, I said, 'Look, even though you are not in the scenes, you are what the audience has to be thinking about.'"

Mostow says he was incredibly glad to have Quinlan in his film:

"She felt very real to me. She was the appropriate age. She didn't feel like some glamorous movie star. She's a very beautiful woman, but she felt authentic."

But the female casting—and thusly the movie—could have turned out very differently. During the pre-production process, when all this casting was occurring, and various studios flirted with the idea of becoming involved, other actresses were mentioned.

"[A studio] said, 'One thing: We want to put such-and-such actress in.'" says Mostow. "It was an actress who, at the moment, was a very huge television star. And a good actress. But she was also twenty years younger than Kurt. I just said, 'Wait a second. This is a guy and his wife, not a guy and his young trophy wife. . . . That's just not what the movie is. If the guy's got a wife like that then that's already a very different guy than this guy. This has got to be a relatable guy.'"

And that wasn't the only way in which an outside contributor almost imposed an unwanted element into Mostow's film.

"Dino, in one the few creative disagreements we had about the movie, he had always felt like you just can't start the movie with two people on the road. You need to have some character development. And so he commissioned a novelist to come and do some writing on the script and do this character development. So this novelist wrote ten pages that tacked on to my script, and came before it. It showed Kurt as a video cameraman during the war in Bosnia. He has this situation where he sees some young girl is going to get shot, but he doesn't say anything. And he winds up accidentally filming it, and he feels guilty about it. He quits his job, and he comes home. His wife picks him up at the airport. They go back home and discuss what they're doing. He decides he's going to make a life change and take this job he was offered across the country in San Diego, and they're going to drive to San Diego.

"This was about ten minutes of stuff. And it had battle scenes, tanks, all this kind of thing."

Mostow said it was "fine writing" but that it was "superfluous." He had it scheduled at the end of shooting, hoping he could eventually convince everyone to scrap these scenes.

Breakdown's trio of nefarious desert villains were portrayed by actors J.T. Walsh, M.C. Gainey and Jack Noseworthy. Mostow says Walsh got the role by auditioning, and Noseworthy said he too auditioned.

Noseworthy's first appearance in the film would require his character to pretend to be developmentally disabled. Even though the character is merely trying to fool Russell's hero, the audience doesn't yet know this, so the mannerisms had to be credible. The actor said he had a pattern for those, thanks to a previous film role.

"I had done this movie, *Barb Wire*, where I played a blind guy," says Noseworthy in a 2011 phone interview. "And I went to this institute for the blind, and I spoke to and worked with some blind people so I could be believable on film. And they also dealt with some mentally challenged people as well. . . . I went and met with and talked to some mentally challenged folks and spent the day in this warehouse, where they get an opportunity to work. And they do things like wrap cans in boxes with cellophane. And they do really basic jobs so that they have a purpose. And I was able to sit down and observe them and go through this day with them."

Walsh, Noseworthy and Gainey are convincing in the film as a small confederacy of miscreants, despite disparate looks and ages. The youngest actor of the group attributes this to extra time spent together before shooting.

"We rehearsed for a couple of weeks, maybe even three weeks," says Noseworthy. "And if I'm not mistaken, Kurt had never really rehearsed a movie for that long. We were in L.A., and we went to a space where we could talk about the guys. We talked about what they were doing and where they were coming from, and kind of developed a sort of camaraderie—with Kurt in tow. That was really advantageous, I think, for the success of the film—that we spent time really rehearsing and talking about characters, similar to what you would do for a play. It's not often you get to rehearse a movie like that."

Mostow doesn't remember those rehearsals, but he does remember an earlier period, during the making of Kurt's previous film, that he and his leading man got to spend one-on-one prep time.

"For the four months before we shot the movie, Kurt was doing . . . *Escape from L.A.*," Mostow remembers. "That movie was all at night, like seventy nights. So Kurt would work Monday through Friday, going to work after dinner and coming back after dawn. And on the weekends [which Russell had off], he would want to keep that schedule, because it's just too grueling to switch back to the day schedule on the weekends . . ."

"So he said to me, 'Look, if you want, you can come over on Saturday and Sunday nights after dinner, and if you don't mind staying up late . . . we'll work all night and just go through the script, because I've got to stay up nights anyway, and I'd appreciate, frankly, the company. So that became what I did for several months."

Principal photography of *Breakdown* occurred in the spring of 1996. The budget has been estimated at $36M (boxofficemojo.com and other internet sources) and at $40M (Mostow).

"We shot in Bartstow, California," says Noseworthy. "And then we shot outside of Las Vegas. I was in Vegas for a while. We would stay somewhere off the strip, and then they'd just pick us up and drive out to a desert location."

Other locations included parts of Utah and Placer County in Northern California. And as for the hangar-like barn that the trucker villain used to dock his semi? It may have seemed credible as the villain's private desert property, but it was actually surprisingly near civilization.

"The barn was one of the few locations inside the Studio Zone," says Mostow. "There were about three weeks of the movie that I actually got to sleep in my own bed in Los Angeles. And that was one of them. That was at a farm that was at the very outskirts of what is called the 'Studio Zone.' There's a point in Los Angeles that's the center of a circle with a thirty-mile radius [around it]. And that's called the Zone."

Whether the locations were remote or not, the production made clever use of them. One scene, for instance, took place on a cliff and had Russell's hero being coerced into a scheme that involved the small desert town below.

"That scene was shot in the desert, but with a huge green screen behind him [Russell] so that they could create the town behind him," explains Noseworthy.

In the *Virginian-Pilot* newspaper interview, Russell described the shoot as having an "us against the wilderness conflict." And Noseworthy confirms that the desert was "hot and dirty" and "sometimes quite windy – the sound guys certainly hated that."

But perhaps *Breakdown*'s biggest production complication resulted from the promises De Laurentiis made to the film's star.

"How it would work is that he would get picked up at seven in the morning," says Mostow of Russell. "He would be driven to Santa Monica Airport near his house, which is a local private airport. A jet would fly him near to wherever we were shooting. We picked locations that were near private airstrips. He would land at the airstrip, which, depending on where we were, could be an hour, an hour-and-a-half flight. So actually, almost two hours for Utah. And when he landed, there would be a helicopter there waiting. The propellors would already be going. He would be hustled from the jet to the helicopter. The helicopter would fly him to the set, which was usually within a ten-minute helicopter ride from the airstrip. He would land right near the make-up trailer. He would go through make-up and then be driven out to where the set was. Keep in mind, these sets were often literally out in the middle of the desert, where we needed we needed a 360-degree vista. . . . He'd arrive, and I'd generally get him for one shot before lunch. Then we'd have to break for lunch. We'd come back, I'd get him for another few hours, and then at about 4:30 in the afternoon, it was like that old TV show *M*A*S*H*; you'd hear the helicopter coming in. We'd know we had to finish up."

For the good of the film, Russell did make an exception to his "home by seven" provision.

"Once we were shooting in Northern California," says Mostow, "we asked if he would please stay just stay one night, which he of course did. But he only had to stay overnight on location once during the whole movie.

"It was when we were shooting in the American River, I don't remember why it was that we needed him to stay over, but I think it was because it was a very complicated day with a lot of rigging, and we needed more than the usual amount of hours that we would get with him."

The severe restriction on the star's shooting availability was mitigated by two things. The first was the nocturnal rehearsal groundwork that had been laid during Russell's *Escape from L.A.* weekends.

"By the time we got to the set, he and I knew what we wanted out of every beat of that film," says Mostow. "There was never any time wasted discussing what a scene was going to be, because we had had all those discussions already."

The other helpful factor was Russell's status as a lifelong film actor, immensely familiar with the process.

"Kurt was an unbelievable pro, so it's rare I that ever shot more than three or four takes," says the director.

The other cast, too, seemed to feel that Russell's commitment compensated for his shorter shooting days.

"You watch Kurt and his professionalism, as he's the lead of the film, and there's never a moment he wasn't giving one hundred percent," says Noseworthy. "Those conditions that Kurt had . . . they were respected, and they were never an issue whatsoever. We knew what our shooting schedule was."

There seems little question whether Russell was entirely present and "in the moment" while working. In fact, he was so much so that, through an unusable take, he helped co-star Noseworthy shape his own menacing performance.

"We were shooting a scene where I had to hold a gun to Kurt," says Noseworthy. "And I remember specifically there was one point: Either I wasn't paying attention, or . . . he must have felt like he had an opening. And just out of nowhere, Kurt just grabbed my gun and got it away from me. And they actually had to stop the scene because that clearly couldn't happen. It was a really good test. It set me on guard. I should never let my guard down. This character would never let his guard down. . . . I don't think Kurt intentionally meant to teach me that lesson. I think he was just playing the scene as the good actor that he was. But because it caught me off guard, it absolutely kept me on my toes for any time I had to hold him in the position where he was a victim."

Also enjoyable to work with was villain actor Walsh, who seemed to prioritize the good of the film over his own career needs.

"He was just one of those great guys," says Mostow. "When we'd shoot a scene, I'd have dinner with him the night before, and he'd come to me with the script, and he'd have various lines [of his] crossed out. And they were huge lines he was crossing out. And he'd say, 'I don't need this. I can act this.' He was really quite extraordinary."

Although De Laurentiis obviously had implicit confidence in his director discovery, that doesn't mean the producer was hands off.

"Dino was there a lot," says Noseworthy. "Looking at the shots, making suggestions and talking to Jonathan. . . . He's a very, very big presence. When Dino was on set, he was definitely having his voice be heard."

During production, *Breakdown* belatedly became a studio film.

Mostow says: "It was only when we were two-thirds of the way through shooting the movie and had cut together some footage that the head of Paramount saw it. And Paramount came in and became the U.S. distributor."

According to De Laurentiis, as quoted in the *Dino* biography, Paramount's Sherry Lansing had heard buzz about *Breakdown* during its production, and requested to see some of it. De Laurentiis showed her forty minutes of edited footage, and the "contract was practically signed" when the house lights came up.

And as for the De Laurentiis-commissioned Bosnia sequence that Mostow objected to in pre-production?

"We're getting closer and closer to shooting it, and I'm just unable to convince anybody that we don't need it," says the director. "So it comes time to shoot it, and I have an ego, so I shoot it well. . . . I'm figuring I'll shoot it, but I'm sure that when people see the movie cut together, they'll realize we don't need it. At this point, Paramount had already come into the movie."

Mostow says he showed the entire movie to the studio, and they loved it. He says that as long as his "stock was high" with

Paramount then, he tried an appeal directly to Lansing. But she wanted the extra material in.

After a successful audience test screening and a round of small tweaks to the film, another test screening was arranged, according to Mostow. But the director had a special request this time.

"I said, 'Do me one indulgence.' We're testing the movie down in Long Beach. I said, 'Get the same theater the next night. Same time. Recruit the same demographic profile you're recruiting for this screening. But I want to show the movie [on the second night], and I'm literally going to just remove the first reel of the movie—just take off the first ten minutes—and just start it with them on the road. . . . At that point everyone was so happy with the movie and happy with me, that they thought, 'All right, we'll indulge this guy even though he's completely nuts on this idea.'"

Mostow says the test screening went very well with the Bosnia footage on the first night.

"[Studio] people are thinking, 'Do we really have to come back the second night?' I said, 'Please, I know it's a pain, but come back.' And Kurt was there both nights too, because he was curious. So everyone comes back . . . the chairman of the studio, all the executives, everybody. And we screen the movie, and as the credits at the end are rolling, everybody walks out to the lobby. And to their credit, they just looked at me and said, 'That's the movie. We don't even want to see the research cards.'"

Mostow says Russell's character, in the final film, is perfectly conveyed to the audience without the war footage.

"Character is not revealed by dialogue. Character is not revealed by [backstory] scenes. Character is revealed by behavior. And Kurt is such a great actor. Everything—the wardrobe he was wearing, the car he was driving, everything about his mannerism, everything about them as a couple—spoke to who he was. And you just got that he was a soft-around-the-middle big-city yuppie."

Breakdown opened in the U.S. in May, 1997 as the number-one film in its first weekend, with a three-day total of $12.3 million. It beat out the other new film of that week, *Austin Powers: International Man of Mystery*. During that same weekend, Mostow's film also bested holdover Hollywood products with bigger spectacle (the disaster film *Volcano* starring Tommy Lee Jones) or top-of-the-A-list talent (Jim Carrey in *Liar, Liar*).

Breakdown received plenty of positive reviews. It was summarized as "A powerfully nerve-racking contemporary thriller," by critic Lisa Schwarzbaum for *Entertainment Weekly*. In the *Chicago Sun-Times*, Roger Ebert praised the film as "taut, skillful and surgically effective." Todd McCarthy wrote in *VARIETY* that *Breakdown* is "a tremendously tense thriller that expertly keeps tightening the screws throughout its taut running time."

The film had its detractors too, even if some of them praised the film in the same breath. Ebert thought the stunt-filled climax was out of place with the earlier part of the film. And Stephen Hunter of *The Washington Post* felt that "[Russell's] lack of energy afflicts the film as much as its director's lack of ideas."

But mostly, *Breakdown* drew repeated, favorable comparisons to Steven Spielberg's *Duel* and to the European thriller *The Vanishing*. (A later movie book by Michael Karol noted that *Breakdown* shared some striking similarities—right down to the diner—with a 1973 TV movie called *Dying Room Only*, which also concerned a spouse going missing when a married couple travels across the desert.)

And the reference points to the story aren't just fictional ones. De Laurentiis' reason for liking the story—its plausibility—was spot on. Shortly after *Breakdown* was released to theaters, the judge in the murder trial against John Famalaro instructed jurors not to see Mostow's movie, as there were too many coincidences to the killing of Denise Huber, who also disappeared after car trouble and who was stored in an ice box.

Breakdown sometimes was reviewed relative to another everyman/fish-out-of-water story, 1972's *Deliverance*, whose rural, degenerate villains were even more extreme. And academic writer Susan Jeffords' essay "*Breakdown*: White masculinity, class and US action adventure films" (that appeared in the 2004 book *Action and Adventure Cinema*) suggests that Mostow's film "narrativize[s] white middle-class fears of the white lower classes." Mostow concedes that the film works on that level, even if it wasn't his intent.

"I think people have certain attitudes and prejudices they project on [other classes], both for the person inside the car looking out, and for the person outside the car looking in. I think the movie just plays on those. And I didn't pursue them in some sort of overt, conscious way. I just wrote from the gut."

Over its run, *Breakdown* was viewed as a commercial hit, bringing in a domestic gross of over $50 million, according to boxofficemojo. com. This U.S. gross alone was far in excess of the film's budget.

Mostow was singled out in many of the reviews, with typical praise like "[he] demonstrates remarkable resourcefulness for a newcomer" (Todd McCarthy, *VARIETY*). When the reviews cited his previous directing credit of the TV movie *Flight of Black Angel*, it reinforced the fact that this truly was a big summer hit movie directed by a relative unknown. Mostow was catapulted into the strata of working Hollywood directors, and in the next decade, he helmed big-budget actioners *U-571* (again working with De Laurentiis), and *Terminator 3: Rise of the Machines* and *Surrogates*. He hasn't forgotten about the opportunity that lead him to his successful career:

"Without Dino's backing, I never would have made [*Breakdown*]. And Dino easily could have said to me, 'Thank you very much, but I'm going to get a different director.' And he didn't do that. He just had this faith in me, and I don't know where it came from. He just bet on his own gut instincts, even when everyone was telling him not to. I owe him everything. It was the kind of thing you just don't see any more in Hollywood."

Mostow, in turn, has shown loyalty, casting *Breakdown* actor Jack Noseworthy again in many of his subsequent projects.

"We just worked really, really well together," Noseworthy says. "At this point, if Jonathan tells me to turn my head right, I turn my head right."

The film was also vindicating for Mostow as a writer, although he understands why the story may not have connected with some entities—studios, actresses, etcetera—in script form.

"It's an interesting thing I found in the suspense genre," says the writer-director. "What is very clear in mind is suspenseful, very rarely do people understand it on the page. And the way that scripts tend to be read in Hollywood is that an executive or an agent goes home and they have a box of twenty scripts that they have to read in a weekend. And they flip the pages quickly because they just want to find out what happens. And that's not how you read a suspense script. You almost have to read a suspense script in real time and ingest the moments. The suspense is what's between the lines; it's not the lines themselves.

"I remember when we had the first cast-and-crew screening, some people from the crew came up and said, 'I had no idea! Wow!' And these were people who worked on the movie. They were there the whole time. . . . Very few people are able to read a suspense script and understand it's suspenseful."

Although *Breakdown* was another hit for Russell during his successful 1990s, the actor's next two films—*Soldier* (1998) and *3000 Miles to Graceland* (2001)—both flopped. Perhaps it was because he didn't strike immediately while the iron was hot. In 1996, after wrapping *Breakdown* and while promoting *Escape from L.A.*, the actor announced he was taking 18 months off and not working again until the scheduled fall '97 production of *Soldier*.

After *Breakdown* was apparently his last major role to be released in his lifetime, actor J.T. Walsh died on February 27, 1998. He died of a heart attack while at the Optimum Health Institute outside San Diego ("a health farm—one of these places you go to get in better shape," according to Mostow). Both Mostow and Noseworthy state that the actor was in fine health when making the movie.

"After he died, I helped put together a memorial service for him," says Mostow. "And we had a screening. We assembled clips from a bunch of his movies—about forty minutes' worth of clips. One-, two-, three-minute long clips from different performances. And by the end of it, people were flabbergasted. You saw the breadth of work he had done, and the characters he had played, and how many of them were stuck in your head. You had forgotten it was him, because he was just that guy who just became the character."

"I think *Breakdown* was the movie that finally made people sit up and take notice of him," continues Mostow on Walsh. "I know his salary went way, way up after that movie. I think that's a sign that at least Hollywood, after that movie, said, 'Wow, that guy has something special.'"

So in the final analysis, how is the film regarded by everyone involved?

"A couple years ago I ran into Kurt in Los Angeles," says Noseworthy in the 2011 interview. "We chatted for a little a bit. And he said more than once he thinks this is one of the best performances he's ever given.

"It was a really tight movie. People who really watch film and are film-ophiles, they remember the film. Yeah, it's definitely a 'You're that guy from . . .' film. I get that a lot. And because I'm really proud of it, I'm always happy to hear it."

Mostow too still gets reactions to *Breakdown*.

"When I run into someone who maybe doesn't know me and they found out that I made that film, that's the film they want to talk about. And they often speak about it in a way that feels like they've just recently watched it, because something about it sticks with them. There's a couple of underlying truths to it that resonate with people."

More books from BearManor.

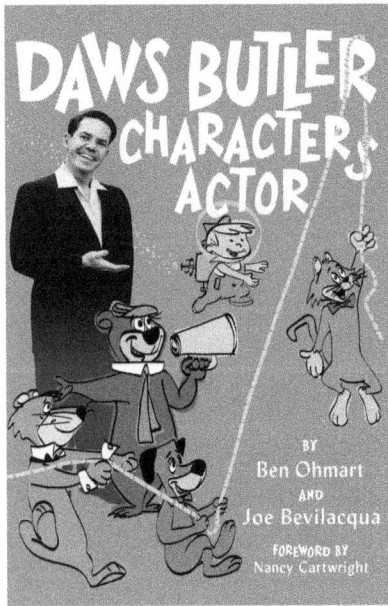

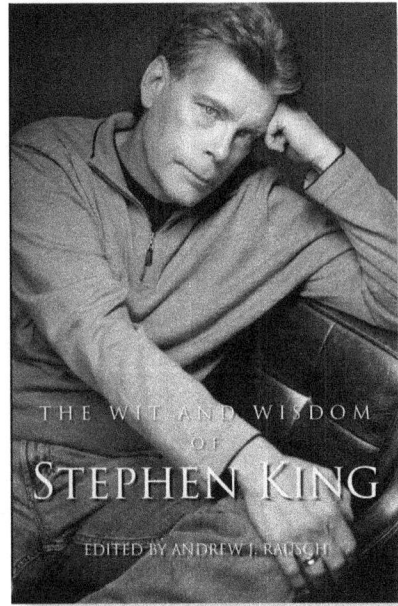

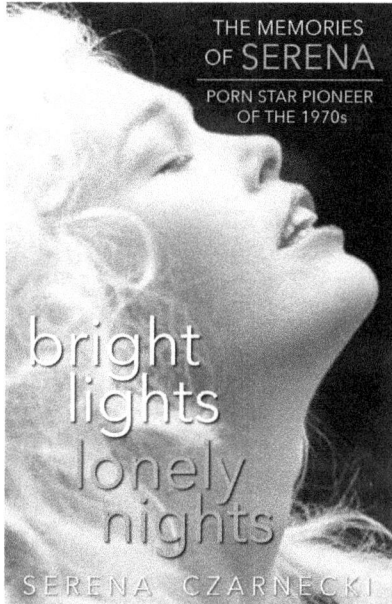

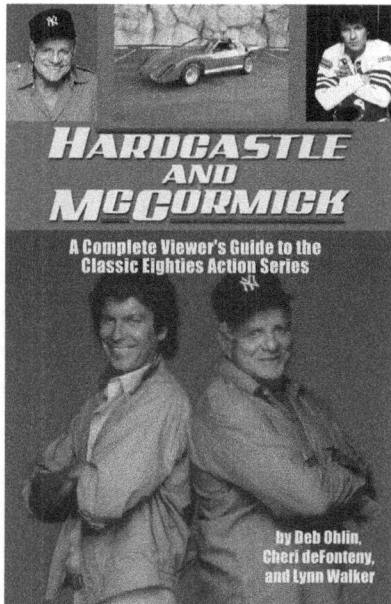

www.ingramcontent.com/pod-product-compliance
Lightning Source LLC
Chambersburg PA
CBHW070806100426
42742CB00012B/2262